MARCO ⊕ POLO

KU-431-573

Travel with Insider Tips

BERLIN

Mecklenburg-Western Pomerania

Schwerin

Elbe

Brandenburg

Lower Saxony

Saxony-Anhalt

Berlin

POLAND

Oder

Hanover

Potsdam

Magdeburg

Leipzig

Dresden

Erfurt

Thuringia

Saxony

www.marco-polo.com

The best Insider Tips → p. 4

INSIDER TIP

Best of ... → p. 6

Sightseeing → p. 26

Food & drink → p. 64

SYMBOLS

INSIDER TIP   Insider Tip

★   Highlight

●●●●   Best of ...

☆   Scenic view

☺   Responsible travel: for ecological or fair trade aspects

(*)   Telephone numbers that
are not toll-free

**PRICE CATEGORIES
HOTELS**

Expensive   over 130 euros

Moderate   80–130 euros

Budget   under 80 euros

Price for a double room,
without breakfast,
in the high season

**PRICE CATEGORIES
RESTAURANTS**

Expensive   over 20 euros

Moderate   10–20 euros

Budget   under 10 euros

Prices based on an average
main course without drinks

On the cover: A stunning island just for art p. 38 | Stay cool at night p. 89

CONTENTS

Shopping → p. 76

Entertainment → p. 86

Where to stay → p. 98

Street atlas → p. 128

MAPS IN THE GUIDEBOOK
(130 A1) Page numbers
and coordinates refer to
the street atlas
(0) Site/address located
off the map. Coordinates are
also given for places that
are not marked on the street
atlas
A public transportation route
map can be found inside the
back cover

INSIDE BACK COVER:
PULL-OUT MAP →

PULL-OUT MAP 〰
(〰 A1) Refers to the
removable pull-out map

The best MARCO POLO Insider Tips

Our top 15 Insider Tips

INSIDER TIP **In memoriam**

Micha Ullman's memorial to the Burning of the Books on Bebelplatz under the Nazi dictatorship draws our gaze downwards. Below the sheet of glass empty bookcases can be seen that symbolise the 20,000 books burned here on 10 May 1933 → p. 31

INSIDER TIP **Asian cuisine**

In the Berlin Mitte quarter, the *Toca Rouge* offers tempting dishes from all over Asia in cool surroundings → p. 75

INSIDER TIP **Telling history**

Former inmates guide visitors through the prison run by the former East German State Security (Stasi) and tell their personal stories of solitary confinement and psychological terror → p. 59

INSIDER TIP **Stalinist glory**

The 90m-wide Karl Marx Allee in Friedrichshain with its monumental, Moscow-style housing blocks was made to impress → p. 37

INSIDER TIP **Paddling in the Spree**

In the *Freischwimmer* restaurant and water lounge (photo right) you can either enjoy the romantic location on the river bank or you can rent a canoe or kayak and explore the Spree. Life jackets available for children → p. 69

INSIDER TIP **Hip design**

The shop *'Aus Berlin'* presents more-or-less useful – and many weird – things created by around 270 Berlin designers. If you are after pills to cure lovesickness, bookends in the shape of pieces of the Berlin Wall or a Television Tower lollipop, this is the place for you → p. 80

INSIDER TIP **A good night story**

The breakfast room doubles up as a library. Readings with famous or still-unknown authors are held regularly in the lounge of the *Literaturhotel* in the suburb of Friedenau. Some literature Nobel Prize winners live(d) just round the corner → p. 101

INSIDER TIP A drink with a view

You can enjoy the magnificent view from the roof of the *Park Inn Hotel* (40th floor) opposite the Television Tower – and sip a cocktail at the same time. There are even deck-chairs waiting for you → p. 101

INSIDER TIP Tempelhof airport

Take a walk along the runways of the now defunct airport and enjoy this open space right in the middle of the city (photo left)! → p. 60

INSIDER TIP 'There ain't much better than a life on a cutter'

The deckhouse of an old stern-wheel tug on the Spree is the perfect place to get your teeth into some sprats or other delights → p. 69

INSIDER TIP Second-hand Beatles

Music fans and vinyl freaks will find 200,000 singles and countless other records at *Platten Pedro*, Berlin's largest antiquarian record shop → p. 78

INSIDER TIP Turkish delights

Try one of the finest Turkish sweets from one of Turkey's best confectioners right in the city centre at the Confiserie *Orientale* → p. 78

INSIDER TIP Sourcing the best

1001 different types of wine line the endless racks along the walls of the *Weinbar Rutz*; the menu is equally global and the cooking is superb → p. 89

INSIDER TIP The BVG's convertible trains

Public transport with a difference: travel the underground in carriages with the roof down – an experience not to be missed! → p. 112

INSIDER TIP Don't get dizzy

The fastest lift in Europe will whisk you to the top of the *Kollhoff Tower* on Potsdamer Platz. There you will not only be able to admire the view but also have a coffee or enjoy your breakfast in comfort → p. 46

BEST OF ...

FOR FREE

● *Lunchtime concerts*

From September to June, you will be able to enjoy a free lunchtime concert every Tuesday in the *Philharmonie*. The performing ensembles are first-rate and include the Berlin Philharmonic and scholarship holders from the orchestra's academy → p. 95

● *Wall art*

The *Eastside Gallery*, the longest open-air gallery in the world, is located to the south of the Ostbahnhof railway station. Take a look at what artists have left for future generations on a 1416 m (4646 ft) long piece of the former Berlin Wall → p. 48

● *Automobil-Forum Unter den Linden*

Prize-winning landscape photographers exhibit their works in the basement of the Volkswagen showroom; highly-prized masters of their art are also exhibited during trade fairs – and it's all free-of-charge → p. 31

● *At the bazaar*

Even though you will probably not need vegetables by the crate load, the 'Turkish Market' on Maybachufer is a real experience. The dealers praise – and bargain over – their goods as if they were in a bazaar in Istanbul. Here you can also try delicious, reasonably-priced, specialities → p. 85

● *Déjeuner sur l'herbe*

In summer, the Berliners pack their picnic baskets and make a pilgrimage to the English Garden in Tiergarten to relax and listen to free concerts of jazz and Klezmer music. Join in the fun! → p. 41

● *Mood indigo*

Egon Eiermann's world-famous new-build is located next to the ruins of the Kaiser-Wilhelm-Gedächtniskirche. Go inside and let the unique atmosphere conjured up by the thousands of blue-coloured glass bricks work on you. The perfect antidote after a shopping spree in the *KaDeWe* or down the Ku'damm → p. 54

●●●● Dots in guidebook refer to 'Best of ...' tips

● *Quadriga with twelve legs*

The Brandenburg Gate (photo) is an absolute must.
Not only the street artists let their hair down here,
there are also many hobby photographers.
Who can take the most beautiful picture of
this city landmark? → p. 41

● *'TV-asparagus'*

This is the name the people of Berlin have
affectionately given the Fernsehturm on
Alexanderplatz. You will really miss out
on something if you don't visit the viewing
platform 203 m (666 ft) above street level –
it's the best view in Berlin → p. 34

● *Wall taxi*

A taxi will take you to all remnants of the Berlin
Wall in the city. The driver will point out the most important places and garnish his stories with his personal ex-
periences in the former divided city → p. 119

● *Curry 36*

Cheap but tasty – that's all a Berlin currywurst needs to be, with some
chips or a bread roll to go along with it. The Berliners queue up at Curry
36 in Kreuzberg for a grilled sausage with curry powder → p. 74

● *Sophisticated shopping*

Time and time again, the *Ku'damm* has been pronounced dead, but the
many customers in the fashionable boutiques on the elegant boulevard
cannot all be wrong. This is where Berlin is at its most glamorous in a
setting of magnificent old buildings: typical of Berlin – but sometimes
beautiful can be expensive → p. 55

● *Don't forget your swimsuit ...*

You will feel like you are at the seaside: deck chairs and sand as far as the
eye can see. The wide expanse of water at Wannsee is an inviting place
to sunbathe or take a swim, and a snack bar is never far away → p. 23

● *Jazz in a beer garden*

Real Kreuzbergers don't give a hoot about the yuppies in Mitte or
Friedrichshain when they sit back with a pint in their hands in one of
'their' beer gardens – listening to live jazz in Yorckschlösschen, for
example → p. 93

BEST OF ...

● *Under water*
The sharks, jellyfish and crocodiles in the *Zoo-Aquarium* become especially popular when it's raining cats and dogs outside. You will find it much more peaceful upstairs among the snakes and tarantulas → p. 56

● *Museum Island*
Fancy the Processional Way in Babylon, a Monet or even Nefertiti? You will be really spoilt for choice trying to decide between the five museums on the Museumsinsel with their magnificent collections → p. 38

● *Expedition to the tropics*
You will feel like you are in a jungle in the tropical plant glasshouse in the Botanical Garden it is so warm and humid among all the palms, ferns and lianas → p. 56

● *In a tent*
The impressive tent-like roof over Potsdamer Platz is not only a protection from the rain. The *Sony Center* (photo) also offers a huge range of open-air entertainment and culinary delights too. The setting is particularly impressive in the evening when the coloured LEDs in the ceiling start to glow → p. 45

● *'Mein Haus am See'*
This is where you can have a cup of coffee, eat a sandwich and sink into the comfy chairs 24 hours a day. Street art on the walls, an international crowd and the underground is only one minute away → p. 67

● *Shop till you drop*
You can easily spend an entire day in the *KaDeWe*, the largest department store on the European continent. Just visiting the delicatessen area is a thrill → p. 82

RAIN

RELAX AND CHILL OUT
Take it easy and spoil yourself

● *Dream away*

You float in salt water and listen to underwater music in a kind of grotto. The sauna, steam bath and massages in the *Liquidrom* next to the Tempodrom are pure bliss → **p. 44**

● *A cup of tea*

Taking part in the Chinese tea ceremony in the *Berghaus zum Osman- thussaft* calms down even the most hectic person. The world's noise simply is left outside the door → **S. 57**

● *Beach bar*

In summer, you can lie back in a deck chair in *Strandbar Mitte* (photo) with a view of the Spree and Bode Museum. In the evening, join in a tango or salsa and indulge in a pizza from the wood-fired oven washed down with a glass of wine or beer → **p. 89**

● *Sweating Turkish style*

Let yourself be pampered in true oriental fashion in the *Sultan Hamam* in Schöneberg – hamam and Turkish massages → **p. 61**

● *Fairy-tale figures*

The water splashing out of fountains and fairy-tale figures is tremen- dously soothing and the fresh air performs miracles. You can regain your stamina at the *Fairy-tale Fountain* in the Volkspark in Friedrichshain → **p. 50**

● *Pfaueninsel*

This idyll on the outskirts of town is easy to reach with the BVG's double deckers and ferries. Wide stretches of grass are the per- fect place to relax or have a picnic, and the peacocks that give the island its name fend for themselves → **p. 58**

● *Fancy a footbath?*

Are your feet tired from all the walking? Then, the *Fußbadcafé* in Mitte is just the place for you! This is where you can take a re- laxing footbath while en- joying a cup of coffee or tea → **p. 67**

INTRODUCTION

DISCOVER BERLIN!

Berlin attracts creative people from all over the world as if by magic. No other city in Europe has as much art and culture to offer! No matter whether it is art, dance, theatre or music, the cultural scene in Berlin provides a stage for international stars and also acts as a breeding ground for talented youngsters to develop their skills and become the real avant-garde themselves. With its more than 150 concert halls, theatres and other stages, three opera houses and around 200 museums and art collections, Berlin has an enormous variety of cultural institutions.

Apart from the Museum Island with its magnificent exhibits, the treasures found in the more than 440 small galleries are equally unique. This has made Berlin one of the most important cities in the art-business world. For the people of Berlin, culture is not merely the State Opera and Philharmonie but also the countless concert clubs and tiny theatres 'round the corner' where superb performances are often held and seats are surprisingly cheap. Berlin is famous worldwide for its feverish nightlife with more than 200 clubs, innumerable bars, cafés and pubs. There are no set closing times and most places stay open until the early hours of the morning – if they close at all. The

Photo: The Reichstag

'in' districts of Mitte, Friedrichshain, Kreuzberg and Prenzlauer Berg, with their varied theatre, club and pub scene, are typical of this metropolis' international orientation.

> **Despite the burden of history Berlin is growing back together again**

Today, you hardly ever get the feeling that this city was once divided by a wall. In the past, however, you didn't need a compass to work out where the East stopped and the West began. The wall that ran through the centre of the city from 1961 to 1989 could really not be missed. In the one half there was East Berlin, the capital city of the German Democratic Republic that came under the influence of the Soviets and, in the other half, the walled-in city of West Berlin under the protection of the western allies France, Great Britain and the USA. Now, more than 20 years after the Fall of the Wall, visitors to the city can barely see the difference in a cityscape that once developed differently as a result of the two political systems. Many of the prefabricated concrete buildings which were typical of the GDR in the eastern part of the ctiy have been revamped. They look so surprisingly modern and cosy that living on the 8th floor of a building on Alexanderplatz is now considered chic. And, when you stand at Checkpoint Charlie – the erstwhile Allied border crossing on Friedrichstraße – you will see that the former eastern sector is dominated by luxurious business premises and boutiques while a certain dreariness has spread across the west.

With a population of around 3.4 million, the new – and old – capital Berlin is still in a period of upheaval. Enormous efforts have been made since the reunification of

Summer in the city – pavement cafés on Kurfürstendamm

Germany to create an architecturally representative capital city. There have been continuous building, restoration and revitalisation activities everywhere. Potsdamer Platz was Europe's largest building site in the 1990s but has since successfully established itself as a new city centre. The Sony Center's tented roof is now regarded as one of the city's new landmarks. Berlin is exceedingly proud of its glass main railway station – Europe's largest – that was opened in 2006. Since 2008, an enormous multi-purpose indoor arena, the O₂ World, in the GDR's former main station – the Ostbahnhof – has drawn huge crowds for pop concerts and the basketball games of the first-division team Alba Berlin. A new office and commercial district is growing up around it. After the demolition of the Palast der Republik, the former seat of the East German parliament, plans are underway for the former royal palace to rise from the ashes and become the home of the 'Humboldt Forum' with museums for non-European cultures and a range of other scientific institutions and libraries.

Even sceptical Berlin residents are proud of the successful architectural solutions devised for the government district. From the dome of the Reichstag you can see to Potsdamer Platz in the south, the monu-

In the new seat of power

mental glass roof of the main station to the north, the Federal Chancellery to the west and the offices of the MPs to the east. Many politicians and their advisers walk to their parliamentary debates and you will be surprised at how many famous people you will come across in the nearby restaurants and cafés. And, there is something else that is only possible in a city like Berlin: first and foremost, people are thought of as people. Whether somebody is famous or not is purely secondary. Live and let live – that's Berlin's motto.

People of 186 nationalities live in Berlin. The dialogue with Eastern Europe in particular has enriched Berlin's cultural life. DJs from Bucharest work the turntables, dance companies from Kiev show their new productions and authors come from Warsaw to promote their books. At least 200,000 Russians and Poles, together with Ukrainians and Czechs live in Berlin where it can be witnessed first hand how a divided country is growing together and how Europe is becoming more unified as well – after all, Berlin is the only capital city in Europe that is located both in the east and west! Many Russians and Ukrainians who have settled in Berlin are Jewish and this has led to everyday Jewish culture once again finding its rightful place in the city. If you stroll around the area near Oranienburger Straße in Berlin Mitte, you will come across a Jewish school and cafés and restaurants serving Jewish and oriental specialities. On the other hand, life in the former western inner-city areas, especially Kreuzberg and Wedding, is characterised by the Turkish way of life. You can see large Turkish families bartering for crates of aubergines and grapes at the markets or discussing things with friends while traders praise their goods at the top of their voices. Quite an experience!

Throughout Berlin's 770-year history newcomers to the city have often brought innovative cultural and artistic impulses with them. Having set up home here, their customs and traditions have left a mark on the city, especially on the culinary sector. *Bouletten* (or *Buletten*) for example is a French word for meatballs that have become a Berlin speciality. In the past, people facing religious persecution in particular were drawn to the Spree as Prussia's regents were known far and wide for their religious tolerance. In 1701, during the reign of Friedrich I, a church was built for the Protestant Huguenots – the French Cathedral – and St Hedwig's Cathedral was built at the end of the 18th century as a Catholic house of worship for the Silesians. In 1886, Europe's largest synagogue – with seating for 3200 people – was opened on Oranienburger Straße. This was destroyed in World War II and has only been partially reconstructed.

Over the years, Berlin has played a central role in world history on many an occasion. Memories of the Nazi dictatorship, the persecution of the Jews and the terrible consequences of World War II are kept alive with countless memorials and remembrance sites. Although the inner city was badly bombed, many historical buildings have now been preserved or reconstructed. The State Opera Unter den Linden, Berliner Dom, the Schauspielhaus, as well as the German and French Cathedrals on Gendarmenmarkt are magnificent examples of this. And, there is the Museum Island with its unique ensemble of stately Classicist buildings with archaeological and art collections that are now all open to the public after the completion of lengthy reconstruction work.

Open spaces add an extra dimension to life in the city

Of course, the recent past has also left its mark. Many of the young people who live in, or visit, Berlin never experienced the divided city themselves. This makes memorials such as the Wall Documentation Museum on Bernauer Straße or the Allies Museum in Zehlendorf even more important than ever before. The drone of a Douglas DC 3, a transport plane from the time of the airlift in 1948/49, when supplies to the western sector of the city had to be masterminded completely from the air as a result of the Soviet blockade, brings back memories of that period whenever it takes off – on special occasions – for flights over Berlin. French, English, Russian and American educational institutions and cultural centres still bear witness to the former presence of the four Allied occupying powers. Some Berlin children visit a French music school while others attend a college with a pronounced emphasis on Russian studies.

The 400,000 trees that were planted along the streets to make life in the walled-in city more bearable when West Berlin was an 'island' have also remained to this day. In fact hardly any other comparable city has as many parks and green spaces as Berlin. And the residents of Berlin are similarly 'green' when they think about the quality of life in their city. More than 43 per cent of all their journeys are made on foot or by bike and 26 per cent use public transport. Only half of all households have a car. An increasing number of visitors to Berlin can now be seen pedalling hard around the city and there are an enormous number of places where bikes can be rented. Berlin is also the secret organic food capital with more specialist shops per head than any other German city.

The only problem is the economy. Dealing with the results of 40 years as a divided city is not as easy to come to grips with as many people had hoped. And progress is

The Neptune Fountain spouts water in front of the Rotes Rathaus

painfully slow. In the past, the city was kept alive under two opposing political systems and, today, Berlin is still finding it difficult to exist without a stable, efficient economy that has evolved over decades. In spite of the rapidly increasing number of jobs in the service sector, Berlin has to live with a current unemployment rate of 12 per cent.

However, the city is making the most of its potential as a base for scientific institutions. The universities, specialist colleges, research and scientific organisations are important employers providing around 200,000 jobs. Business in the creative sector is also booming – especially in the IT field and

The perfect place for the adventurous and creative

design branch. In turn, this has had a positive effect on trade exhibitions as well. The world's leading specialist trade rair for street and urban wear *Bread & Butter* is held in Berlin. Even stars like Justin Timberlake show their fashion labels here and, with a turnover of around 100 million euros, *Bread & Butter* generates an important economic impulse. Time and time again people from Berlin have been successful in establishing themselves as avant-garde businesses and product designers. There are ideas everywhere, but Berlin is where they become reality. And you may well feel the same as many local residents who, despite seeing their city day in, day out, continuously discover exciting new things around about and are often surprised at how much they didn't know before. Berlin is like a lucky-dip – you never know what you're going to come across next!

WHAT'S HOT

1 What takes your fancy?

'I did it my way' Put your own meal together. At *Mamo Falafel* oriental sandwiches are made the way you want (*Warschauer Str. 47,* photo left). Fish, vegetable sprouts or chilli? *Shabuki* is the place where you can choose the ingredients you want in your soup. If you want to combine this freedom of choice with the comfort of your home, go to the 'walk-in recipe book' of *Kochhaus Schöneberg.* They will sell you the recipe AND all you need to prepare it. Tasty and so practical *(Akazienstr. 1, www.kochhaus.de)*!

Balancing act 2

Well balanced? It is hard to imagine life in Berlin's parks without them: the slackliners. You just have to keep your head up and your arms out, a foot or so off the ground. You can buy all you need from *Globetrotter (Schlossstr. 78–82)* or *Peak Outdoor (Wilhelminenstr. 88).* If you don't want to walk alone, you can find kindred spirits in the *Berliner Slackliner Community* (photo right).

Creative stronghold

3

Potsdamer Straße From a problem district to a creative stronghold. The renowned Galerie Klosterfelde has already opened at *93 Potsdamer Straße (www. klosterfelde.de)*. The house next door, number 91, is now the premises of the *Freies Museum (www.freies-museum. com,* photo). And, if you believe all the creative folk, the district will continue to flourish. Patricia Kohl and Salome Sommer, who have recently moved into the neighbourhood with their gallery, are making the most out of what was once a bed factory and the creative audience in the vicinity *(Kurfürstenstr. 13/14, www.sommerkohl.com)*.

(Electro)mobile in Berlin

Like a rocket People in Berlin like to be on the move – but not if the environment has to pick up the bill. Then they swing themselves onto an electric *erockit* motorbike. It is driven by muscle power – but also has a built in 'amplifier'. Your own energy gets multiplied by 50! The faster you pedal, the faster the bike goes – and makes conventional bikes at the crossing look like real antiques (photo right). In 2012, a field study started in the capital in which hybrid and electro cars were included in the Deutsche Bahn's car-sharing programme. The *BeMobility 2.0 (www.bemobility.de)* project wants to make this environmentally-friendly step possible for Berlin residents. The infrastructure is there and, with around 100 battery charging stations, Berlin is a real pioneer in this field.

4

Action speaks ...

5

... louder than words The *Haus der guten Taten* ('Good Deed House') really lives up to its name. The welfare organisation sells products made in special workshops by handicapped people; the profits flow back into social projects *(Coeo, Schlossstr. 1 | www. coeo-berlin.de)*. The *Guerrilla-Gardeners* come armed with bulbs and rakes. Their aim? To beautify the city and green public spaces for the benefit of all – and, if there is a need, this can even be in a building skip or at the former airport (*www.guerillagardening. org, www.facebook.com/SmilingGarden*, photo right).

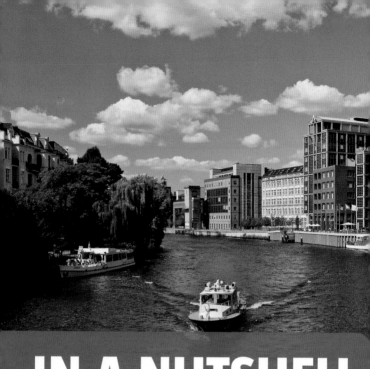

IN A NUTSHELL

ALTERNATIVE CULTURE

Off theatres with 99 seats, small hip clubs and concert venues in hidden courtyards: you can discover Berlin's real charm if you venture beyond the highly-subsidised cultural palaces. Only those who have been to a performance in the *Theater zum Westlichen Stadthirschen* (Western City Deer Theatre) or listened to a punk band in *Schokoladen* (Choc Shop) will know what this means. This is where locals and newcomers have fought for some cultural freedom to make it possible for them to experiment with new kinds of performing arts way off the beaten track. This is where you can get a close-up view of the origins of new movements in music, theatre and art! Berlin's nightlife always has something novel to offer: the trendy clubs in abandoned buildings or old factories are often not officially registered; their addresses are passed on almost on the sly. The best way to find out what is going on is to ask a local or look at Facebook. Once you have got your hands on one of these secret addresses you'll be the proud owner of a piece of insider information – but only for a short time. Like nomads, most of the clubs soon move on to a new location.

ART METROPOLIS

With its more than 440 galleries and numerous collections, Berlin is one of the most important art markets in the world.

Bars on the banks of the Spree, the rebuilding of the royal palace, the charm of East Germany in your hotel room – anything is possible

Collectors fly in regularly to buy new works. Street art is also of major importance. Compared to the total number of residents, Berlin has the largest percentage of freelance artists in Germany – six per cent. This number has increased by more than 40 per cent since 2000 – partly due to the fact that it is comparatively cheap to rent studios. And – unlike in Paris, London or New York – even young artists can live comfortably in Berlin.

BERLIN PALACE

Severely damaged in World War II, its ruins blown up on the orders of the East German authorities, the royal palace originally on this site is now about to rise from the ashes. After the demolition of the Palast der Republik, East Berlin's former cultural centre, a green area with wooden benches around the edge now offers visitors a view of the Fernsehturm. In 2017, the reconstruction of the royal palace's façade will begin. Inside, there will be space for the *Humboldt Forum* housing a number of museums focusing on non-European cultures, the State Library and collections owned by Humboldt University.

COURTYARD ARCHITECTURE

Berlin is famous for its collection of courtyards. It is not at all rare to find between two and eight blocks of flats, one behind the other, connected by courtyards and passageways. This style of architecture, typical to Berlin, has led to the Hackesche Höfe in Berlin Mitte regaining its former fame. Other examples of skilful courtyard redevelopment in Berlin Mitte are the Heckmann-Höfe on Oranienburger Straße, the Sophie-Gips-Höfe on Sophienstraße and the Kurt-Berndt-Höfe on Neue Schönhauser Straße. The latter was built for the Metropol Palast Company in 1911/12. After being given back to its former owners, the building was remodelled and modernised in the late 1990s.

DEMONSTRATIONS

Berlin is not only the seat of government but also where Germans like to protest. Roughly seven demos are registered daily. Yet among them are reoccurring events such as the march in remembrance of the socialist leaders Rosa Luxemburg and Karl Liebknecht in January, several 1 May demos and the gay and lesbian parades on Christopher Street Day, are regular occurrences.

On some days, the traffic in the city has a hard time; this can be the case when farmers drive their tractors into town to protest against agricultural polices while, at the same time, students take a stand against the austerity programme of the State of Berlin and parents hold a rally for free kindergarten places for their children in front of the Town Hall.

DESIGN

Unesco has recognised Berlin as a 'City of Design', making it the first German city to be included in a global network of creative centres, the 'Creative City Network', founded by the organisation. Other member cities in this illustrious club include Buenos Aires, as another 'City of Design', and Edinburgh as a 'City of Literature'. Currently, nine educational institutions, including two art academies and three fashion schools, provide training for designers and, according to the Economic Senate, around 5500 students are taking advantage of these offers. Approximately 8000 designers and artists are actively involved in the creative sector where they produce all sorts of things from furniture to coat stands, lamps and works of fine art. In Berlin, artists and designer firms generate a turnover of approximately 800 million euros a year – a growing market that is acknowledged internationally. The branch's showcase event is the annual *DMY International Design Festival Berlin (www.dmy-berlin.com)* with exhibitions and experimental designs focusing on a specific subject.

DIALECT

'They don't mince their words' is one of the most common explanations for the – frequently, quite brusque – rhetoric of the locals from Berlin. If you get on a bus and ask the driver the best way to somewhere, be prepared for a stroppy answer ('Do you think I'm an information office, or something?'). There are definite limits to friendliness; but if you don't take the gruff exterior too seriously and have a quick-witted riposte on hand, you will soon be accepted. Although you might already know some words in German, remember: in Berlin bread rolls are called *Schrippen* not *Brötchen*, and doughnuts are definitely not *Berliners* but *Pfannkuchen*.

FASHION

The trend scouts of the major fashion firms regularly come to Berlin to get inspiration from the imaginative, daring outfits worn by those living in the 'in' districts Mitte, Prenzlauer Berg and Friedrichshain. The fashion fairs *Bread & Butter* and *Premium* have played a major role in promoting fashion design. Some Berlin designers sew one-off garments in backrooms and sell them out front. But the man on the streets does not pay much attention to fashion. Most people in Berlin are more interested in being comfortably dressed. And in some districts you could almost believe that tracksuits and flip-flops are considered chic …

GREEN, GREENEST

Berlin residents really know how to save energy. According to statistics, they produce less CO_2 per inhabitant than anywhere else in Germany! And only every second household – that means every third resident – has a car! Several large companies and state institutions, including the federal buildings and German Bundestag, obtain their heat from power stations fired with vegetable oil and their water is warmed by solar energy. The federal headquarters of the Christian Democratic Party and the new premises of the Green Party's Heinrich Böll Foundation are also equipped with photovoltaic panels. If you are interested, you can take a tour in a solar boat *(tel. 0151 54 22 80 44 | www.solarpolis.de)* to become acquainted with the sights and buildings from the water – and save energy at the same time. Many locals also try to make sure that their groceries are organic and come from the region. Countless large and small organic markets are flourishing although, compared to the average in Germany, the net household income in Berlin is rather modest. The largest organic supermarket is located on

The Orient on the Spree – Turkish weekly market in Kreuzberg

Senefelderplatz in Prenzlauer Berg and has a total retail area of almost 17,000 sq ft. Its nutrition-conscious customers are drawn by 18,000 different products including 200 different wines and 180 varieties of cheese.

LOVE OF ANIMALS

People in Berlin seem to be crazy about anything on four legs. Dogs in particular are real favourites and pedestrians always have to look at least one step ahead to avoid treading on a 'stinking landmine'. But dog poo is not the only problem; our canine friends simply do not have enough space to run about in. The legal exercise areas in the Volkspark in Friedrichshain and Hasenheide in Kreuzberg are notoriously overcrowded. That not everybody is capable of dealing with his becomes clear if you visit the animal shelter on the north-eastern outskirts of the city. Covering an area of 40 acres – including a pet cemetery – it is the largest of its kind in Europe. As many as 12,000 animals are cared for by a staff of more than 100 every year.

MAJOR AIRPORT

There is no end to the squabbling over the expansion of Schönefeld Airport to create a new major airport. After more than 20 years of planning and construction, there is still no end in sight and the people of Berlin are already manning the barricades to protest about flight paths. South Berlin will be especially subjected to aircraft noise. Local residents rightly fear not only a decrease in their quality of life but also in the price of their property. Their neighbours in the north, on the other hand, can heave a sigh of relief. The closure of Tegel Airport means that, after 40 years, it has now become possible to sleep more peacefully in Spandau and Reinickendorf.

MULTICULTURAL

People from 186 nations can be found in Berlin. Some streets – particularly in Neukölln, Kreuzberg, Moabit and Wedding – are dominated by Arab and Turkish culture. But, life in the city would not be the same without the supermarkets, bakeries, cafés and restaurants of the Russians (mainly in Charlottenburg and Marzahn), Poles and the workers formerly contracted to help out in East Germany – the Vietnamese. Unemployment is especially high among migrants. Many Turks who came to Berlin as immigrant workers more than 40 years ago found themselves out of work after the Reunification of Germany and factories and firms closed down one after the other. There are hardly any jobs for unskilled workers without a school leaving qualification and it is disastrous that almost 12 per cent of the young people from migrant families living in Berlin are unable to start an apprenticeship because they lack this basic qualification. The Berlin Senate is attempting to solve this problem through new education campaigns such as making it compulsory to attend a day-care centre with special language training before starting school.

ON THE WATERFRONT

Hardly any other city in Europe is blessed with as many lakes, rivers and canals as Berlin. There are more than 500 km (310 mi) of shoreline where you can go for a walk, sunbathe and even live! Most of the restaurants and clubs with a view of the water are located near the Oberbaumbrücke in Friedrichshain. Beach bars with deck chairs on the shores of the Spree and, of course, a vast number of places where you can swim in summer – all boasting a water quality standard from good to excellent – invite you take a break. A highlight is the more than 100 year old
● *Strandbad Wannsee (April–Oct daily*

Why would residents of Berlin need to go to the Mediterranean when they have the Wannsee?

10am–6 pm, in summer until 8pm | admission 4 euros | www.strandbadwannsee. de | S 1, 7 Nikolassee), Europe's biggest continental see and swimming bath. Guests get the feeling of being at the Baltic Sea with its fine sand and wicker beach chairs with a hood.

OSTALGIA

Everyday East German culture became absolutely trendy at the very latest when Wolfgang Becker's cult film 'Goodbye Lenin!' was released in 2003. Design articles from the former state-owned enterprises (VEB) are now highly sought-after: shops with Mitropa tableware and GDR furniture almost have to drive away prospective buyers. And those who feel like spending a night in an original GDR bed can have this wish fulfilled in the prefabricated-concrete *Ostel* Hotel near the Ostbahnhof. However, one should not forget that there are two sides to every coin: a visit to the Stasi prison in Hohenschönhausen brings back memories of the many negative aspects of the regime. Former political prisoners guide you through the building and give personal accounts of the solitary confinement and inhuman interrogation methods practiced here.

SCIENCE

Did you know that Berlin is one of the leading cities for science in Europe? Around 200,000 scientists, students and other specialists teach, study and carry out research in four universities, the Charité Medical University, eight specialist colleges, three art academies, 18 private universities and more than 60 research institutes. Every year in June, they join up forces and organise an evening of events that gives an interesting insight into the achievements of individual institutes and research centres.

THE PERFECT DAY
Berlin in 24 hours

08:30am **BREAKFAST**

The best place to start the day is in *Käfer's roof-garden restaurant* → p. 67 at the top of the *Reichstag* → p. 47 (advance reservation essential). From here, you will have a magnificent view over the inner city and can also follow the spiral walkway up into the dome of the building.

09:30am **POLITICS AND HISTORY**

Hire a Segway at *Potsdamer Platz* → p. 45 and zoom around the centre of Berlin on one of these fun, electrically powered 'personal transporters'. The perfect route: Leipziger Platz, then turn left into Wilhelmstraße, cross the boulevard Unter den Linden and carry on just before reaching the Spree. Turn left there. Keep going passed the Reichstag on through the government quarters. Feel like a coffee? Then drive in the direction of the main railway station to the Gustav-Heinemann-Brücke. Take the stairs that lead down to the Spree along the bridge to the Capital Beach (don't forget to lock up the Segway). After that, keep zooming in the direction of the *Brandenburger Tor* → p. 41 and you'll find yourself back on Potsdamer Platz again.

11:30am **LUNCH IN A CONSUMER'S PARADISE**

Bus no. 200 will take you past the diplomatic district to the *Gedächtniskirche* → p. 54, the former symbol of West Berlin at the end of Kurfürstendamm. *KaDeWe* → p. 82 is just a stone's throw away. Take a lunchtime break on the gourmet floor in the traditional department store and later take a closer look at the enormous selection in the delicatessen, clothing and perfume sections, to name just three.

01:30pm **ART OR STREET LIFE?**

How about a tour of Kreuzberg? The bus M 29 will take you there. Get off at Görlitzer Bahnhof and take a stroll past the mad mixture of bars, boutiques and döner kebab stands between Oranienplatz and Wiener Straße (photo right). On 'Görli'work your way down Oranienstraße, Kreuzberg's Ku'damm, and you will come across many shops selling fashion items by Berlin designers as well as Turkish bakeries. Or how about a bike ride around Prenzlauer Berg with its mass of cafés, 'in' shops and the *Kulturbrauerei* → p. 48? Bikes can be hired from

Discover the best of Berlin – the very essence of the city – in a relaxed way in just one day

companies such as *Berlin on bike (Knaackstr. 97 | tel. 030 43 73 99 99 | www.berlinonbike.de)* in the Kulturbrauerei.

`03:30pm` AROUND 'ALEX'

The U2 (Eberswalder Straße stop) takes you from the Prenzlauer Berg and the U8 from Kreuzberg to the *Alexanderplatz → p. 34*. The 'Alex' main attraction is the Berlin *Fernsehturm → p. 34* with its 203 m (666 ft.) high viewing platform. Take the express lift and let it catapult you up the 'Telespargel' (TV-asparagus), as the locals call it, in 40 seconds. Or enjoy – somewhat cheaper but not as high – the great view from the terrace on the 40th floor of the *Park Inn Hotel → p. 31*.

`04:30pm` CULTURE ON THE ISLAND

From there, it is just a stone's throw to the Schlossplatz with the new *Humboldtbox* and the *Museumsinsel → p. 38* (photo) – the mecca within Berlin's museum landscape. Art-lovers will not only be fascinated by the first-rate collections on display in the Old and New Museums, the Pergamon and Bode Museums, as well as the National Gallery, but also by the meticulously restored buildings themselves. But, don't try to do too much at once; come back a second or third time when you have a few more hours to spare.

`07:00pm` NOSTALGIC DINING AND SUNKEN LINERS

In the 'East German restaurant' *Domklause → p. 71* on the banks of the Spree you can end the day with dinner and sample what the political elite enjoyed tucking into in the self-styled 'Socialist state of workers and farmers'. After packing in so much into one day, you may well be looking forward to a well-earned nightcap: the

Start: Reichstag/Unter den Linden
Public transport: S1, 2, 25;
bus 100, M 41
Best time to start: in the morning

place to head for is *Riva Bar → p. 88*, located under the arches of the district line railway. The bar in the shape of the sunken luxury liner *Titanic* is unique and the drinks can also be recommended.

SIGHTSEEING

WHERE TO START?
Alexanderplatz (133 F2–3)
(*L3–4*) is the ideal place to start your visit of Berlin and it is easy to reach by underground (U 2, 5, 8) or on the district line (S 3, 5, 7, 75). The entrance to the public car park for 600 vehicles is off the central strip on a level with Alexanderplatz 6. The Rotes Rathaus, the seat of the Lord Mayor of Berlin, is also right on 'Alex' and it's just a short walk to reach the Museum Island with the Cathedral, the Pergamon and Bode Museums and many other institutions.

Even Berliners sometimes have difficulties recognising certain parts of their city. Those who haven't been into the city centre for several months will find new buildings have popped up on what were empty pieces of land, new bridges have appeared where there was no crossing before, and newly-opened museums waiting for them to explore. No other European city is changing so quickly!

The construction boom has also taken hold of the western sector of the city; new hotels are springing up everywhere, rundown buildings on Kurfürstendamm – such as the famous Kanzlereck – have simply been demolished and modern structures have taken their place. The airy buildings in the

Photo: High rise buildings on Potsdamer Platz

Berlin is changing at a breathtaking pace. New museums, whole streets and buildings make the city like a fascinating kaleidoscope

government district never fail to captivate viewers and visitors have to queue up patiently to see inside the Reichstag with its glass dome. But, there is still plenty of scope for inspired architecture and new ideas. First and foremost, there is the Ostbahnhof where a new commercial district has been built. And then there is the reconstruction of Berlin's former royal City Palace; the Palast der Republik that replaced the Baroque edifice on the site has already been demolished. The new residential and office district that is being developed near the Main Station, the largest in Europe, that was opened in 2006, is also worth a visit. The inner city is gradually starting to show itself at its best and anybody who walks through the restored Brandenburg Gate today will find it difficult to believe how desolate Pariser Platz behind it was for so many years. Many visitors see a city that didn't exist in this form 15 years ago

The map shows the location of the most interesting districts. There is a detailed map of each district on which each of the sights described is numbered.

and don't even notice it. Whether on Potsdamer Platz or Friedrichstraße, the architects have been successful in at least one aspect: the post-modern architecture has been assimilated perfectly into the cityscape almost everywhere and only a few make fun of the fact that Berlin still does not have a skyscraper. The residents of Berlin prefer to keep things within reasonable limits and there is still not enough economic power to warrant a business district like the one in Frankfurt am Main. On the other hand, culture ranks very highly in Berlin. With over 200 museums, collections and archives, Berlin has a superlative museum landscape. Painting, everyday culture, technical and local history – there is such a great variety that it would take months even to get some sort

of general overview. And, on top of that, there is always something new.

The courage to take cultural risks has a long tradition in Berlin. Does any other city have a museum specially built for an excavated altar? It is not without reason that the Pergamon Museum, opened in 1930, is one of the most popular in the city and attracts around 1 million visitors annually. And that can be said about the entire Museum Island, too. The ensemble of five museums houses artistic treasures that can only be matched worldwide by the Louvre in Paris and the Hermitage in Saint Petersburg. It was Crown Prince Friedrich Wilhelm came up with the idea of a centre for art and history. The *Old Museum* (Engraving Collection), the *New Museum*, *Bode Museum* and *National*

Gallery (European and German 19th century painting) and *Pergamon Museum* (Collection of Antiquities, Middle-Eastern Museum, Museum for Islamic Art, Main Archives and Library) developed between 1825 and 1930. The New Museum has been remodelled to plans by the British architect David Chipperfield and, since autumn 2009, is home to the collection of the Egyptian Museum which was formerly displayed in the Old Museum. The Bode Museum, with its impressive dome, presents exhibits from the Museum for Byzantine Art and sculptures.

The *Stiftung Preußischer Kulturbesitz* (Prussian Cultural Property Foundation) developed out of Friedrich Wilhelm III's 'royal museum' and now includes the Berlin State Museums, State Library, Secret State Archives and the Ibero-American Institute, as well as the Institute for Music Research with its Musikinstrumenten-Museum. The latter has its home in the Culture Forum in Tiergarten, the West Berlin counterpart to the Museum Island. Entrance fees to the Berlin State Museums range from 4 to 8 euros but considerably higher prices are charged for special exhibitions such as those at the Neue Nationalgallery. Information on all museums, guided tours and special exhibitions: *tel. 030 24 74 98 88* or *www.museumsportal-berlin.de.*

MITTE

The treasures on Museum Island are considered highlights from the history of art by experts around the world, the Television Tower with its viewing platform way above everything else is a real crowd-puller on sunny days, and taking a photo of the city's most important landmark – the Brandenburg Gate – is a must.

MARCO POLO HIGHLIGHTS

MITTE

Mitte's cultural heart: Berliner Dom on Museum Island

Mitte has, by far, more sights than any other district of Berlin. Take a walk along Unter den Linden and you will discover the historical heart of the city. The Humboldt University, for example, where famous scientists such as Albert Einstein and Rudolf Virchow taught. Or the Armoury with the German Historical Museum. There is also plenty of action in the evening between Gendarmenmarkt, the Nikolai District and Neue Synagoge: the restaurants, bars and clubs will make sure that you'll enjoy yourself until the early hours. The best place to go shopping is around the Hackescher Markt. That is where Berlin designers have set up their studios and shops. Modern art is mainly sold north of the Neue Synagoge; the density of international galleries is quite impressive.

damaged in World War II. The main section of the building only became available for services in the mid-1990s after extensive reconstruction work had been completed. The altar with the Apostle Wall, the baptismal font and two candelabras are still from the old cathedral. The Hohenzollern crypt is the resting place for around 90 monarchs and members of the Prussian nobility. There is a INSIDER TIP wonderful view of the Museum Island and Site of the palace from the ☀ dome! *April–Sept Mon–Sat 9am–8pm, Sun 12noon–8pm; Oct–March Mon–Sat 9am–6pm, Sun 12noon–7pm | entrance fee 7 euros | prayers Mon–Sat 12–12.30pm, Mon–Fri 6–6.30pm, services Sun 10am, 6pm | several tours daily | Am Lustgarten | www.berliner-dom.de | S 3, 5, 7 Hackescher Markt | bus 100 Schlossplatz*

▌1▐ BERLINER DOM (133 E3) (*Ø K–L4*)

The cathedral, constructed between 1894 and 1905 under the supervision of the architect Julius Carl Raschdorf, was severely

▌2▐ INSIDER TIP COMPUTERSPIELE-MUSEUM (146 A2) (*Ø N4*)

An oversized Atari joystick, the first 3-D glasses and lots of game consoles can be tried. 300 exhibits spread over an area of 600 m² (0.15 acres) document the 40 year history of the digital game culture from Pong to Zelda. *Wed–Mon 10am–8pm | admission 8 euros | Karl-Marx-Allee 93a | www.computerspielemuseum.de | U 5 Weberwiese*

▣ DDR MUSEUM (133 E3) (*ᗰ L4*)

Those that actually experienced it have mixed feelings about this review of everyday life in East Gemany with its restricted range of food, tacky jeans, nudist holidays, Erika typewriters and music by Karat and City that can be heard once again over headphones. The history of life in the GDR over more than 1000 m². *Daily 10am–8pm, 10pm on Saturday | entrance fee 6 euros | Karl-Liebknecht-Str. 1 | Spreepromenade | www.ddr-museum.de | S 3, 5, 7 Hackescher Markt*

▣ INSIDER TIP ▶ DENKMAL DER BÜCHERVERBRENNUNG (133 D4) (*ᗰ K4*)

This memorial on Bebelplatz near the State Opera created by the Israeli artist Micha Ullman commemorates the Burning of the Books on 10 May 1933. Works by Erich Kästner, Bertolt Brecht, Kurt Tucholsky and other authors who the Nazis did not approve of were flung onto the fire. The memorial in a former tram tunnel is conceived as a cleared out library with room for 20,000 books. You look into the empty bookcases through a sheet of glass in the ground. *Unter den Linden | bus 100 Staatsoper*

▣ DEUTSCHES HISTORISCHES MUSEUM (133 D3) (*ᗰ K4*)

The core of the permanent exhibition that was reopened in the Armoury in 2006 is formed by the so-called 'epoch rooms'. The visitors wander through them from the beginnings of German history to the present. Temporary exhibitions are shown in the new building designed by Ieoh Ming Pei. *Daily 10am–6pm | entrance fee 6 euros | Armoury (old building) | Unter den Linden 2 | www.dhm.de | S 3, 5, 7 Hackescher Markt*

▣ DOROTHEENSTADT CEMETERY (138 A6) (*ᗰ J–K3*)

Many of the greats from the world of art and culture have found their final resting place here. Among them are the former Federal President Johannes Rau, Heinrich Mann, Bertolt Brecht, Helene Weigl, Anna Seghers, Heiner Müller, Karl Friedrich Schinkel, Johann Gottlieb Fichte and Georg

LOW BUDGET

▶ Free exhibitions by prize-winning natural photographers as well as special shows of quality works of art are presented in the basement of the VW-Showroom in the ● Automobil-Forum **(132 C4)** (*ᗰ K4*). *Daily 10am–8pm | Unter den Linden 21 | Mitte | U/S Friedrichstraße*

▶ You will have a trip past many of the sights in Berlin for the price of a bus ticket by simply taking bus no. 100 from Bahnhof Zoo to Alexanderplatz. Stops at the Siegessäule, Schloss Bellevue, Reichstag and Brandenburger Tor.

▶ There is a magnificent view over the city from the ⚡ roof of the *Park Inn Hotel* **(133 F2)** (*ᗰ L3*) (*daily 12noon–10pm, from 3pm in winter | Alexanderplatz 7 | Mitte*) on Alexanderplatz. Entrance to the panorama terrace on the 40th floor is only 3 euros.

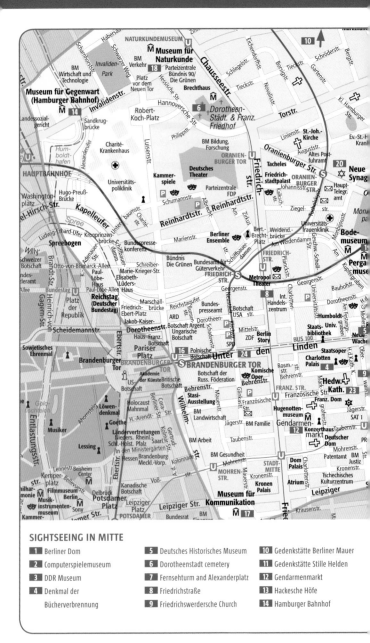

SIGHTSEEING IN MITTE

1 Berliner Dom
2 Computerspielemuseum
3 DDR Museum
4 Denkmal der
   Bücherverbrennung

5 Deutsches Historisches Museum
6 Dorotheenstadt cemetery
7 Fernsehturm and Alexanderplatz
8 Friedrichstraße
9 Friedrichswerdersche Church

10 Gedenkstätte Berliner Mauer
11 Gedenkstätte Stille Helden
12 Gendarmenmarkt
13 Hackesche Höfe
14 Hamburger Bahnhof

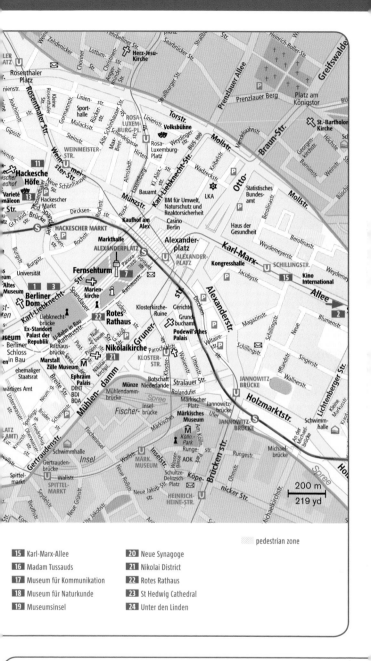

pedestrian zone

World-time clock at the base of the Fernsehturm on Alexanderplatz

Wilhelm Friedrich Hegel. The remains of the French cemetery that was set up for the Huguenots in 1780 can also be found within the walls. The old trees make this a quiet spot to escape from the mad rush of the city and catch your breath. *Chaussee-straße 126 | U 6 Naturkundemuseum*

7 FERNSEHTURM AND ALEXANDERPLATZ ★ ☼
(133 F2–3) *(ᗰ L3–4)*

This edifice is the second highest television tower ● in Europe and one of the city's landmarks. Built between 1966 and 1969, the tower with its glass sphere and overall height of 365 metres can be seen from almost everywhere in the centre of the city. It is hard to find a place on the platform 203 m (666 ft) above the ground on cloudless days. An SMS service makes it possible for you to not have to queue or wait: visitors are sent an SMS when it is their turn. Then the express lift will catapult you up to the platform in a mere 40 seconds. The restaurant *Sphere* (tel. 030 24 75 75 37 | Moderate) above the viewing platform revolves around its own axis twice an hour. If it is a clear day, you will be able to see a good 40 km (25 mi). *Nov–Feb daily 10am–midnight, March–Oct 9am–midnight | entrance fee 12 euros, VIP ticket 19.50 euros (no waiting time!) | Panoramastr. 1a | www.tv-turm.de Alexanderplatz* at the base of the television tower (on the other side of the railway tracks) was named in honour of Tsar Alexander I in 1805 and formerly used as a parade ground and market. Today, it is

ment store renovated, and *C&A* moved into the listed Berolinahaus completed in 1929. Only the *World-time Clock* and *Friendship between Nations Fountain* bring back memories life in former East Berlin. The *Neptune Fountain* is located near the Rotes Rathausl: the god of the sea, balancing with his tripod – this has led to the nickname of 'fork basin' – on a large shell seems to want to get a better view of things. Stretched out beneath him are four female figures representing the Rivers Oder, Weichsel, Rhine and Elbe. He was only given this place near the Town Hall after he was restored in 1969. *Alexanderplatz | U/S Alexanderplatz | bus 100 Spandauer Straße*

8 FRIEDRICHSTRASSE
(132 C1–6) (*ϕ K4–5*)

Friedrichstraße was already the place to go for some fun in the 1920s. The street, some 3.5 km (2 mi) long, that crosses the Mitte district from north to south is lined with theatres, cabarets and bars. Before the Reunification, the Berlin Wall cut the street in two and the border crossing here was the famous Checkpoint Charlie. Today, there are only a few sandbags piled up high and a control booth to remind you of this. Stylish business premises, such as

overrun with people on a shopping spree and visitors to the television tower. The square completely changed its appearance after it was restored, the *Kaufhof* depart-

BERLIN ON THE WATER

The most pleasant way to discover the historic Mitte or government districts is by taking a cruise. Numerous ships chug up and down the Spree all year long. The stops include the Museumsinsel, Friedrichstraße and the Haus der Kulturen der Welt. A round trip from Mitte via Kreuzberg to Charlottenburg and back to Mitte along the Spree and Landwehr Canal is particularly interesting. On this three-hour tour you will not only see most of the main sights in the city, the onboard 'cityscape guide' will also give you lots of information about the everyday life and customs of the people of Berlin. *Information on sailing times and prices: tel. 030 5 36 36 00 | www.sternundkreis.de.*

Always busy: the pubs and cafés in the Hackesche Höfe

the *Quartier 206* with its exclusive boutiques, now dominate the skyline. The *Galeries Lafayette*, with its glass atrium, is another architectural highlight. The *Friedrichstadtplast* was already famous for its revues when this area was still part of East Germany. *U/S Friedrichstraße*

◼9 FRIEDRICHSWERDERSCHE CHURCH (133 D4) (𝄜 K4)

Karl Friedrich Schinkel created one of the major German, neo-Gothic works with this church that was built between 1824 and 1830. Statues from the early 19th century line the interior. The main focus is on Classicist sculptures by Johann Gottfried Schadow, Christian Daniel Rauch and other artists of the period. *Daily 10am–6pm | entrance free | Werderscher Markt | U 2 Hausvogteiplatz*

◼10 GEDENKSTÄTTE BERLINER MAUER (132 A4–5) (𝄜 K2)

A section of the original wall has been left standing. Observation slits let you get a glance of 'the other side'. This makes it pos-sible for visitors to gain an impression of the divided city. An exhibition in the documentation centre gives information on everyday life on Bernauer Straße in the walled city that is no longer in Mitte but already part of the district of Wedding. *Tue–Sun April–Oct 9.30am–7pm, Nov–March 9.30am–6pm | entrance free | Bernauer Straße 111 | www.berliner-mauer-dokumentationszentrum.de | S 1, 2 Nordbahnhof*

◼11 GEDENKSTÄTTE STILLE HELDEN (133 E2) (𝄜 L3)

This impressive archive uses multimedia technology to present the biographies of Jews and those who protected them in the Third Reich. *Daily 10am–8 pm | entrance free | Rosenthaler Str. 39 |www.gedenkstaette-stille-helden.de | S 3, 5, 7, 75 Hackescher Markt*

◼12 GENDARMENMARKT ★ (133 D4–5) (𝄜 K4)

With its buildings from the 18th and 19th centuries this is considered the most beautiful square in the city. The

Schauspielhaus, which was built by Karl Friedrich Schinkel between 1818 and 1821 and now serves as a concert hall, and the Schiller Monument are framed by the Französische and Deutscher Dom. The *French Cathedral (Tue–Sat 12noon–5 pm, Sun 11am–5pm | entrance to the tower 2.50 euros, Huguenot Museum 2 euros | Gendarmenmarkt 5)* suffered severe damage during the war and was reconstructed in 1983. It was built between 1701 and 1705 for the 8000 Huguenots living in the city at that time. An exhibition in the cathedral provides an informative description of the life of these Calvinist Protestants.
The 70 m (230 ft) high tower was built from 1780–85 and you have a magnificent view over the historical heart of Berlin from the top. The *German Cathedral* at the opposite side of the square is no longer used as a church today but as an exhibition space on German history. *U 6 Stadtmitte*

13 HACKESCHE HÖFE
(133 E2) (*M L3*)

The Hackesche Höfe were built between 1905 and 1907 and this labyrinth of interconnecting courtyards has since become an architectural highlight. Restaurants, cinemas, galleries, a cabaret and boutiques have been set up in them. Many Jews used to live in the neighbouring Sophienstraße with its long tradition as a centre of craft and retail businesses. The partially restored *New Synagogue* (p. 39) on Oranienburger Straße bears witness to this area's past. *S 3, 5, 7, 75 Hackescher Markt*

14 HAMBURGER BAHNHOF
(143 E1) (*M J3*)

The former railway station has been transformed into a museum with a total area of 140,000 square feet where especially art from the past 60 years is on display; most of the works were provided by the collector Erich Marx. The core of the collection is formed by works by Robert Rauschenberg, Roy Lichtenstein, Andy Warhol, Cy Twombly, Anselm Kiefer and Joseph Beuys and added to this an excellent permanent loan from the Flick Collection are shown in special exhibitions. *Tue–Fri 10am–6 pm, Sat 11am–6pm | entrance fee 8 euros, special exhibitions 12 euros | Invalidenstr. 50 | www.hamburgerbahnhof.de |S 5, 9, 75 Hauptbahnhof*

15 INSIDER TIP KARL-MARX-ALLEE
(145 D–F 2–3) (*M M–O 3–4*)

Not only the architecture of this boulevard, the longest listed ensemble of its kind in Germany, points towards Moscow. Socialist realism, also called the 'Stalinist gingerbread style', can be seen on both sides of this impressive road built between 1952 and 1960 that is nearly 90 m wide. Only rubble was left of what was once Frankfurter Straße after the war. The symbol of this impressive avenue, with its housing blocks that are nearly 300 m long and up to 9 storeys high, are the two towers at Frankfurter Tor that were modelled on the towers of the cathedrals on Gendarmenmarkt. The buildings were mainly built using the rubble of bombed houses. On 17 June 1953, the worker's revolt that was brutally crushed flared up on this street which was called 'Stalinallee' until 1961. *U 5 Frankfurter Tor*

16 MADAME TUSSAUDS BERLIN
(132 B4) (*M J4*)

The famous wax museum near Brandenburg Gate has around 80 life-sized models, ranging from Berlin's Lord Mayor Klaus Wowereit to Johnny Depp, Madonna and The Beatles, football stars and Angela Merkel. *Daily 10am–7pm | entrance fee 20.95 euros, online ticket 19 euros (Tip: tickets are as much as 5 euros cheaper* from the BVG ticket machines!) | Unter den Linden 74 | www.madametussauds.com | U/S Brandenburger Tor

17 INSIDER TIP MUSEUM FÜR KOMMUNIKATION
(132 C6) *(ω K5)*

The Museum for Communication is considered the oldest postal museum in the world. Since its renovation (1996–2000) the visitor is presented with a fascinating exhibition including a computer gallery, interactive exhibits, robots, Philip Reis' first telephone apparatus and the most famous stamps ever: the red and the blue Mauritius. *Tue 9am–8pm, Wed–Fri 9am–5pm, Sat/Sun 10am–6pm | entrance fee 3 euros | Leipziger Str. 16 | U 2, 6 Stadtmitte*

18 MUSEUM FÜR NATURKUNDE
(143 F1) *(ω J3)*

This collection with more than 25 million zoological, paleontological, mineralogical and geological objects is world class. After its restoration, the famous INSIDER TIP original skeleton of the Brachiosaurus brancai – 23 m (75 ft) long and 13 m (43 ft) high – can once again be seen in all its glory. Hundreds of specimens provide an overview of our indigenous fauna. *Tue–Sun 9.30am–6pm | entrance fee 6 euros | Invalidenstr. 43 | www.naturkundemuseum-berlin.de | U 6 Naturkundemuseum*

19 MUSEUMSINSEL ●
(133 D–E 2–3) *(ω K–L 3–4)*

Greek and Roman art and sculpture is shown in the *Old Museum*. Etruscan art, the collection's highlight, will not be on display until after the completion of the building's renovation. Until then the Greek works are being exhibited on the main floor. Stone sculptures and figures made of clay and bronze, friezes, vases, gold jewellery and precious silver will make you fully aware of the magnificence of this culture.

The restored *Bode Museum*, with its splendid collection of sculptures, the Museum for Byzantine Art (with pictures from the early medieval period until the late 18th century) and collection of 500,000 rare coins, is the pride and joy of Berlin's residents.

After extensive restoration, the *National Gallery*, with its valuable paintings and sculptures from the 19th century, is now one of the most beautiful museum buildings in Berlin. Works by artists such as Menzel, Schadow and Blechen tell us a lot about the architecture, fashion and spirit of the Imperial period.

The ★ *Pergamon Museum* was built between 1910 and 1930 specifically to house the Pergamon Altar that the engineer Carl Humann had discovered in Turkey in the 19th century and spent 20 years restoring. The sculptural frieze, 113 m (370 ft) long, is one of the great masterpieces of Hellenist art and shows the battle of the gods against

the giants. The majestic market gate from Milet (130 AD), a showpiece of Roman architecture, can be seen in an adjacent hall. The collections of Islamic and Near-Eastern art are also unique in the world. The almost 100-foot long tiled Processional Way of Babylon with its ornate depictions of lions is simply outstanding.

Since 2009, the world-famous, more than 3000-year-old, bust of Nefertiti has been on display in the *Neues Museum* along with the Egyptian collection of the Prussian Cultural Property Foundation. The museum, which is one of the city's loveliest, was reconstructed and combined with modern elements to plans drawn up by David Chipperfield. The museum, built by Friedrich August Stüler between 1843 and 1855 was severely damaged in World War II and remained empty for 60 years. The partially restored wall paintings inside are another highlight.

All museums daily 10am–6pm, Thu until 10pm, Nationalgalerie closed on Mon, Neues Museum Sun–Wed 10am–6pm, Thu–Sat 10am–8pm | www.smb.museum | S3, 5, 7, 75 Hackescher Markt

20 NEUE SYNAGOGE (133 D2) (*∅ K3*)
When it was consecrated in 1866, this was the largest synagogue in the world with seating for 3200 people. Today, the building on Oranienburger Straße is only used for exhibitions and as a place of prayer. Once you have passed through security, you will find yourself in front of a large glass wall which gives you a view of the former place of worship – today, this is a gravelled, open space. The synagogue was only saved from being burned to the ground on the 'Night of Broken Glass' on 9 November 1938 by the courageous intervention of a Berlin policeman. In 1943, a bombing raid almost completely destroyed it. The façade and

The steps of the Pergamon Altar in the Pergamon Museum are a popular place to take a rest golden dome, with a staircase leading up to it, were renovated in 1988. *March–Oct Sun/Mon 10am–8pm, Tue–Thu 10am–6pm, Fri 10am–5pm (to 2pm on Friday in March and October), Nov–Feb Sun–Thu 10am–6pm, Fri 10am–2pm | entrance fee 3.50 euros, dome 1.50 euros Oranienburger Str. 30 | www.cjudaicum.de | S 1, 2, 25 Oranienburger Straße*

21 NIKOLAI DISTRICT
(133 E–F 3–4) (*Ⓜ L4*)

The *Nikolai Quarter* with the Nikolai Church to the south-east of Alexanderplatz is considered the birthplace of the city; this is where the first houses were built in the 13th century. At first glance, it appears that the buildings there today were constructed in the 18th and 19th centuries but most of them were actually built in the 1980s. *U 2 Klosterstraße*

22 ROTES RATHAUS (133 F3) (*Ⓜ L4*)

You can see the red-brick building that was built between 1861 and 1870 on Alexander-platz from afar. The main building is in the style of the Italian Renaissance while the bell tower is modelled on Laon Cathedral in France. Thirty-six panels depicting the history of Berlin can be seen on the first floor. The town hall suffered severe damage in World War II and became the seat of the East Berlin Council in 1958, the Senate of West Berlin taking up office in Schöneberg Town Hall. Since the Reunification of Germany, the Red Town Hall has once again become the seat for all Berlin. *Rathausstr. 15 | tel. 030 902 60 | www.berlin.de | U/S Alexanderplatz*

23 ST HEDWIG CATHEDRAL
(133 D4) (*Ⓜ K4*)

At the beginning of the 18th century there were only 700 Catholics in Berlin. This increased to around 10,000 just 30 years later. They had fled to liberal Berlin in the wake of the Silesian Wars and, for that reason, the foundation stone for a new church, designed by the architect Jean Legeay together with the royal building director Johann Boumann the Elder, was laid in 1747. It was not until 1773 – almost 30 years after building had started – that the Baroque church could be used. It is modelled on the Pantheon in Rome. The cathedral suffered severe bomb damage in World War II but was reconstructed relatively quickly (1952 to 1963). *Mon–Sat 10am–5pm, Sun 1pm–5pm | Bebelplatz | U 2 Hausvogteiplatz | bus 100 Staatsoper*

24 UNTER DEN LINDEN ★
(132–133 B–D 3–4) (*Ⓜ J–K4*)

The boulevard, which begins at *Brandenburger Tor* and ends at *Berliner Dom*, has still not lost any of its importance as Berlin's intellectual and artistic centre – this is not least due to the Museum Island. Starting in the 18th century, this was the site of the *Crown Prince's Palace*, the *Armoury*, as well as the *State Opera* and

Pedestrians and cyclists on Unter den Linden

today's *Humboldt University*. At the end of the 19th century, Berliner Dom was constructed in the Wilhelmine style. The boulevard was completely devastated during World War II. With the exception of the royal City Palace which the East Berlin city council had blown up in 1950, all other buildings have been restored or replaced. The palace on the banks of the Spree was replaced by the *Palast der Republik*; during the East German era this was an important national cultural centre but the locals nicknamed it 'Palazzo Prozzi' (Posers' Palace). It has now been demolished and it is planned to reconstruct the former royal palace on its original site. The information centre *Humboldtbox* provides information on the building site and shows a INSIDERTIP model of the city centre. *U/S Brandenburger Tor*

TIERGARTEN

Joggers' favourite park, parliament buildings and a shopping paradise – hardly any other district is as varied as Tiergarten.
You have the best panoramic view of the city from the dome of the Reichstag building from where you can see the striking tented roof of the Sony Center on Potsdamer Platz and the Quadriga, the chariot that crowns Brandenburg Gate. To the west, the golden goddess Victoria on Victory Column beckons over the treetops. Berlin's 'green lung' – the zoo and park – which give this district its name, not only offers the city's stressed residents recreation but also cultural highlights such as the Philharmonie and ● INSIDERTIP concerts in summer in the English Garden or Indian pop bands in the House of Cultures of the World.

1 BAUHAUS-ARCHIV (143 D5) (*Ø H5*)
Fascinating collection on the history of the Bauhaus: furniture, works of art, buildings and objects designed by Ludwig Mies van der Rohe, Walter Gropius and others. Gropius designed the museum in 1964. *Wed–Mon 10am–5pm | entrance fee Sat–Mon 7, Wed–Fri 6 euros | Klingelhöferstr. 14 | www.bauhaus.de | bus 100 Lützowplatz*

2 EMBASSY DISTRICT
(142–143 C–D 4–5) (*Ø G–H5*)
Many embassies have been re-established to the south of the Tiergarten. Diplomats lived here before World War II but only the Japanese and Italian embassies still keep up the tradition from that time. The new embassies of Sweden, Norway, Iceland, Denmark and Finland are architectural highlights in their own right. They share a building complex (Embassies of the Nordic Countries) that also has a community house, restaurant and exhibition rooms. The Mexican Embassy next door, on the other hand, is an avant-garde building with a 18 m (60 ft) high foyer, a rooftop garden and a spectacular façade. All of these embassies consider a cultural programme that is available to the general public as being particularly important and organise regular exhibitions, concerts and readings. *Embassy of the Nordic Countries (Community House Mon–Fri 10am–7pm, Sat/Sun 11am until 4pm | Rauchstr. 1 | tel. 030 5 05 00 | www.nordicembassies.org); Embassy of the United States of Mexico (exhibition hall Mon–Fri 9am–1pm | Klingelhöferstr. 3 | tel. 030 2 69 32 30 | portal.sre.gob.mx/alemania) bus 100 Nord-Botschaften*

3 BRANDENBURGER TOR ★ ●
(132 A–B4) (*Ø J4*)
A million spectators cheered when Berlin's landmark was unveiled on 3 October 2002 after years of restoration work. The people of Berlin are really attached to the emblem of their city that, by the way, never actually served as a city gate. The

20 m (66 ft) high monument has adorned Pariser Platz since 1791; it was built to plans by the architect Carl Gotthard Langhans be removed and a staff with a wreath of oak leaves placed in the Goddess of Victory's hand. Only after the

The four horses on Brandenburg Gate pulling the Goddess of Victory's chariot

who took the Acropolis in Athens as a model. The Goddess of Victory, driving her four horses onwards, is regarded as the harbinger of peace.

After his successful campaign, Napoleon humiliated Berlin in 1806 by taking the Quadriga back to Paris. It was not until eight years later, after the War of Liberation, that it was returned to its original location. Victoria was decorated with an Iron Cross, laurel wreath and Prussian eagle in memory of the battle against Napoleon. Brandenburg Gate was severely damaged during World War II and the city administrations of East and West Berlin used old plaster models to create a copy of the Quadriga. However, the East German government insisted that the Iron Cross and Prussian eagle

Reunification of Germany could the old symbols be reinstated. *Pariser Platz | U/S Brandenburger Tor*

▪️ DENKMAL FÜR DIE ERMORDETEN JUDEN EUROPAS

(132 A–B 4–5) *(𝄞 J4)*

The Holocaust Memorial was inaugurated in May 2005. Following plans drawn up by the New York architect Peter Eisenman, 2711 rectangular columns of various heights, called steles, were set up in rows covering an area of just over 4½ acres. You can enter the complex from all sides and its wave-like shape is perceived differently from wherever you are. A detailed and moving exhibition in the underground information centre *(April– Sept Tue–Sun 10am–8pm, Oct–March*

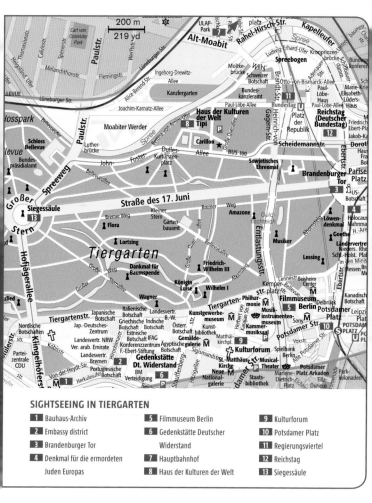

SIGHTSEEING IN TIERGARTEN

1. Bauhaus-Archiv
2. Embassy district
3. Brandenburger Tor
4. Denkmal für die ermordeten Juden Europas
5. Filmmuseum Berlin
6. Gedenkstätte Deutscher Widerstand
7. Hauptbahnhof
8. Haus der Kulturen der Welt
9. Kulturforum
10. Potsdamer Platz
11. Regierungsviertel
12. Reichstag
13. Siegessäule

10am–7pm) is a must. *Wilhelm-/ Behrenstraße | www.holocaust-mahnmal. de |U/S Potsdamer Platz*

5 FILMMUSEUM BERLIN
(132 A6) *(ΩJ5)*

Costumes, posters, photos and excerpts from films from the beginnings of German cinema to the present day are on display. Modern film animation, special effects and virtual worlds are just some of the core themes. You will be able to take a look at old series and quiz shows in the affiliated INSIDER TIP Television Museum. *Tue–Sun 10am–6pm, Thu to 8pm | entrance fee 6 euros | Potsdamer Str. 2 | tel. 030 300 90 30 | www.deutsche-kinemathek.de | U/S Potsdamer Platz*

⑥ GEDENKSTÄTTE DEUTSCHER WIDERSTAND (143 D5) (*∅ H5*)

A permanent exhibition gives an impressive insight into how individuals and groups struggled against the Nazi dictatorship and made use of the limited possibilities they had. *Mon–Wed, Fri 9am–6pm, Thu 9am–8pm | entrance free | Stauffenbergstraße 13 | www.gdw-berlin.de | U 2 Mendelssohn-Bartholdy-Park*

⑦ HAUPTBAHNHOF (143 E2) (*∅ J3*)

The largest station in Europe was built to designs by the Hamburg architectural practice gmp (Gerkan, Marg und Partner). Glass and steel are the main elements of the imposing multi-storey building with its many shopping malls and underground tracks running from north to south. More than 1000 trains pass through here every day. *Europaplatz | U/S Hauptbahnhof*

⑧ HAUS DER KULTUREN DER WELT (143 E3) (*∅ H4*)

This former congress hall was erected for the 1957 Building Exhibition and aroused international interest with its daringly curved roof that led to Berlin residents giving it the nickname of the 'pregnant oyster'. The building has been used by the Federal Government as the 'House of the Cultures of the World' since 1989. Its culture festivals and events focussing on individual countries have underscored its high international reputation. *John-Foster-Dulles-Allee 10 | www.hkw.de | bus 100 Haus der Kulturen der Welt*

⑨ KULTURFORUM (143 E 4–5) (*∅ H5*)

All museums: *entrance fee 8–10 euros | www.smb.museum | U/S Potsdamer Platz* Several of the most important works of European painting from the 13th to 18th centuries are united in the *Gemäldegalerie (Tue–Sun 10am–6pm, Thu to 10pm | Stauffenbergstr. 40)* opened in 1998. The individual artistic landscapes and epochs are presented in 72 main rooms and smaller exhibition spaces. The main focus of the collection is on Italian painting from the 14th to 18th centuries (including works by Caravaggio, Botticelli and Raphael) and 15th and 16th century Dutch art. Treasures from Baroque art and curiosity cabinets are displayed in the *Kunstgewerbemuseum (closed until 2014 due to extensive renovations | Tiergartenstr. 6)*, with Delft faïence and Baroque glass being just two of the highlights of the collection. European porcelain – especially Meissen and KPM – decorative utensils and tableware from the

LEAN BACK AND RELAX

The ● *Liquidrom (Sun–Thu 10am–midnight, Fri/Sat 10am until 1am | day ticket 29.50 euros | Möckernstraße 10 | Kreuzberg | tel. 030 2 58 00 78 20 | www.liquidrom-berlin.de | U 1, 7 Möckernbrücke)* in the Tempodrom **(139 F6)** (*∅ J5–6*) not only scores with its unique architecture. You can float weightlessly in a saltwater tub in a kind of grotto and listen to the dulcet tones of the water that coloured lights turn all colours of the rainbow. In the evening, DJs work the turntables at the edge of the pool – the music ranges from classical to downbeat. Other attractions: the sauna and steam bath, the Balinese herb temple and hot-stone massages.

The heart of Potsdamer Platz: the Sony Center

Rococo, Classicist and Jugendstil periods, gold and silver articles as well as costumes and silks can also be marvelled at.

Around 800 of the more than 3000 European musical instruments from the 16th to 20th centuries in the collection have been on display in the *Musikinstrumenten-Museum (Tue–Fri 9am–5pm (Thu to 10pm), Sat, Sun 10am–5pm | entrance fee 4 euros | Tiergartenstr. 1)* since 1984. The ensemble of wind instruments from St Wenzel zu Naumburg from the first half of the 17th century is absolutely unique, as is one of Bach's harpsichords. You can even try out some instruments and there is a performance on the more than 70-year-old Wurlitzer cinema organ every Sunday at 12noon.

20th century European painting and sculpture, ranging from classical modern art to the 1960s, is the main focus of the exhibition in the *Neue Nationalgalerie* *(Tue–Fri 10am–6pm (Thu to 10pm), Sat/Sun 11am–6pm | Potsdamer Straße 50)* that is housed in a low building designed by Mies van der Rohe. Let yourself be fascinated by the works of Ernst Ludwig Kirchner, Pablo Picasso, Paul Klee, Lyonel Feininger, Otto Dix, Oskar Kokoschka and other masters. Particular emphasis is placed on Cubism, Expressionism, the Bauhaus and Surrealism.

⑩ POTSDAMER PLATZ
(132 A–B6) (*ØJ4*)

This new complex in the heart of the city with a shopping centre, cinemas, a musical theatre, casino, hotels and film museum on the west side of Potsdamer Platz was first opened in 1995 – the original buildings on the site were bombed flat during World War II. The tent-like roof Helmut Jahn designed for the ★ ● *Sony Center* is absolutely stunning. Depending on the weather, this is the perfect place for people-watching or for simply sitting on one of the café terraces. In the *Kollhoff Tower*, Europe's fastest lift propels visitors up to the ✳ INSIDERTIP viewing platform *(daily 10am–8pm; to 6pm in winter | 5.50 euros)* with a panorama café *(www.panoramapunkt.de)* 93 m (305 ft) above the ground in a mere 20 seconds. *U/S Potsdamer Platz*

⬛ REGIERUNGSVIERTEL
(132 A–B 3–4) (𝄞 J4–5)

A string of modern government buildings has sprung up to the west and east of the Reichstag. Plans for the Federal Chancellery to the northwest were drawn up by the architects Axel Schulte and Charlotte Frank who were also responsible for the overall plan of the government district. Its box-like design has led to the Chancellery becoming popularly known as the 'Federal (or Chancellor's) washing machine'. The four interlinked arms of Eduardo Chillida's 18-foot-high steel sculpture 'Berlin' in front of the portal symbolise German unity.

The *Paul Löbe House* to the north of the Reichstag building was named after the Reichstag President in the years 1924–32. It has 21 conference halls and 550 rooms for the 275 members of parliament and their staff.

Its counterpart on the other side of the Spree is the *Marie Elisabeth Lüders House*. It was named after a Reichstag representative, is currently being expanded and houses the Parliament Library – the third largest of its kind in the world. The so-called *Ministers' Garden* to the northeast of Potsdamer Platz, where several of the federal states have their delegations, is also architecturally interesting.

Architecture for the 21st century: the office buildings for the members of the Bundestag

12 REICHSTAG ★

(132 A3–4) (*M J4*)

The glass dome, added to the Reichstag building that was originally built by Paul Wallot between 1884 and 1894, has made it a real crowd-puller. Visitors have to register in advance, in writing, with the *Bundestag* for a tour or reserve a table in the *Käfer Restaurant* on the roof if they want to enjoy a walk up the spiral slope inside the ﹌ dome. From up there, you have a fantastic view over the government district, the main railway station and the rest of Berlin. The panorama is particularly spectacular after nightfall. Down below, members of the German parliament hold their debates and you can watch them at work through the glass roof. The Reichstag was set ablaze in 1933 and severely damaged in battles to regain control of Berlin. It was reconstructed between

1961 and 1972 to house the exhibition on German history, now on display in the German Cathedral. In 1990, the first parliament of a reunified Germany was constituted here. The architect Norman Foster's plans for the building led to it being gutted and crowned with a glass dome to make it suitable for its modern-day purpose. *Visits to the dome currently only by appointment at least 2 hours in advance (on the doorsteps possible, too) | Bundestag Visitors' Service (guided tours and visits to plenary sessions) | tel. 030 22 73 00 27 | www.bundestag.de, link: visit the bundestag | Platz der Republik | bus 100 Reichstag*

13 SIEGESSÄULE (142 C4) (*M G4*)

The 67 m (220 ft) high national monument once adorned the square in front of the Reichstag. In order to have more space for his 'Reichshauptstadt Germania', Hitler had the golden statue of Victoria – who is affectionately known as 'Gold Else' – moved to the Große Stern in Tiergarten. The Victory Column was designed by Heinrich Strack to commemorate the victory over the Danes and erected between 1864 and 1873. There is a fine view of the city from the ﹌ observation platform. *April– Oct, Mon–Fri 9.30am–6.30pm, Sat, Sun 9.30am–7pm, Nov–March, Mon–Fri 10am– 5pm, Sat/Sun 10am–5.30pm | entrance fee 2.20 euros | Straße des 17. Juni | www. monument-tales.de | bus 100 Großer Stern*

PRENZLAUER BERG/FRIED-RICHSHAIN

There are more organic-ice cream shops here than anywhere else and, in summer, the playgrounds are so crowded you will feel like you are in China.

It comes as no surprise that statistics show that the districts of Prenzlauer Berg and Friedrichshain are among those with the most children in Europe. You will see large numbers of young people – not least, because of the exciting nightlife. Hardly anywhere else in the city will you find as many bars, reasonably-priced restaurants, clubs and inns. Students and an increasing number of well-heeled professionals live in Friedrichshain, and Prenzlauer Berg has long been one of the preferred residential areas for highly paid academics. Many of the inhabitants of the two districts flock to the Volkspark in Friedrichshain on weekends to chill out, skate, go for a walk or have a game of beach volleyball.

Pavement cafés on Kollwitzplatz

■1 EASTSIDE GALLERY ●
(146 A4) (*∅ N5*)

The largest open-air gallery in the world stretches from the Ostbahnhof to Oberbaum Bridge. 118 artists from 21 countries have immortalised themselves here on 1316 m (4318 ft) of Berlin Wall. The best-known works are 'Brotherly Kiss' by Dimitri Vrubel and Gerhard Lahr's 'Berlin–New York'. *Friedrichshain | Mühlenstraße | www.eastsidegallery.com | U/S Ostbahnhof*

■2 KOLLWITZPLATZ
(139 D4) (*∅ L–M2*)

Avoiding almost complete destruction, this ensemble of houses around the square is one of the loveliest groups of historical buildings in Berlin. The square was named after the painter and graphic artist Käthe Kollwitz who lived here with her husband from 1891 to 1943. A monument created by the sculptor Gustav Seitz in 1958, modelled on a self-portrait of the artist, acts as a memorial to the famous resident. Many other prominent people live or have lived on Kollwitzplatz, which is also known for its weekly market and its many cafés and restaurants. *Prenzlauer Berg | Mühlenstraße | U2 Senefelderplatz*

■3 KULTURBRAUEREI (139 D4) (*∅ L2*)

The former Schultheiss Brewery has established itself as the district's cultural centre. The courtyard ensemble that stretches over 6 acres is alive day and night thanks to its large cinema, its halls for concerts and other events, as well as any number of clubs, restaurants and shops. The building, constructed in yellow brick that is so typical of Berlin, was erected between 1890 and 1910 to plans drawn up by the royal architect Franz Schwechten who also designed the Kaiser Wilhelm Memorial Church.

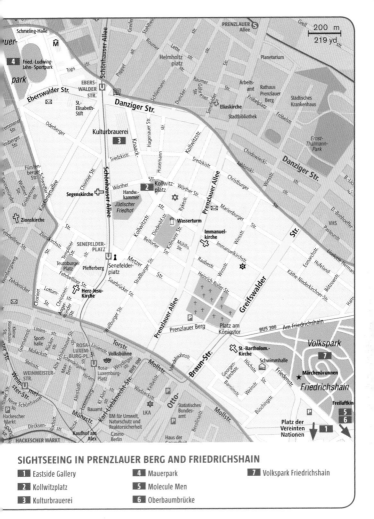

SIGHTSEEING IN PRENZLAUER BERG AND FRIEDRICHSHAIN

1 Eastside Gallery

2 Kollwitzplatz

3 Kulturbrauerei

4 Mauerpark

5 Molecule Men

6 Oberbaumbrücke

7 Volkspark Friedrichshain

*Prenzlauer Berg | Knaakstr. 75–97 | U 2
Eberswalder Straße*

4 MAUERPARK
(132 B–C3) (*Ⓜ K–L 1–2*)

Many dogs and many more adults and children have a great time in this park on what used to be the border between East and West Berlin. Today, graffiti artists try out their talents on a remaining piece of the Wall. The highlights are the gigantic swings to the south and the children's farm at the north end. On Sundays in summer karaoke shows pull the crowds.
*Prenzlauer Berg | Eberswalder Straße | U 2
Eberswalder Straße*

5 INSIDER TIP MOLECULE MEN
(146 B5) (*ᗞ O6*)

Since 1999, the *Molecule Men* have stood in front of the 'Treptowers', the Allianz Group's twin towers. The 30 m-high figures in the Spree created by the American artist Jonathan Borofsky are intended to symbolise peaceful coexistence at this point where Friedrichshain, Treptow and Kreuzberg merge. *Eichenstraße | S Treptower Park*

6 OBERBAUMBRÜCKE
(146 B4) (*ᗞ N5*)

The most beautiful bridge in Berlin, with its elevated railway tracks, street and covered walkway over the Spree, unites the 'in' districts of Friedrichshain and Kreuzberg. It is considered a masterpiece of 19th century architecture and was constructed for a trade exhibition in 1896. The name 'Oberbaum', or 'upper barrier', comes from the days when customs officials blocked shipping lanes here with a barrier so that they could collect their tolls. The Spanish architect Santiago Calatrava designed the new middle section when the bridge was renovated in the 1990s. *Friedrichshain | U 1 Schlesisches Tor*

7 VOLKSPARK FRIEDRICHSHAIN
(145 E–F 1–2) (*ᗞ M–N3*)

The 128-acre Volkspark Friedrichshain in the north is where young people go to race their skateboards through the half-pipe while their parents and younger brothers and sisters relax or play near the ● INSIDER TIP *Fairy-tale Fountain*. Not only children love this fountain that was first filled with water in 1913; nine arches frame stone bowls with cascades, characters from Grimm's fairy tales and balustrades with animal figures. The fountain, with its wonderfully kitschy flair, has developed into a hip meeting place for the eternally young, for families and courting couples. *Friedrichshain | bus 142, 200 Am Friedrichshain*

Oberbaumbrücke: once the border between East and West, now simply one of Berlin's most beautiful bridges

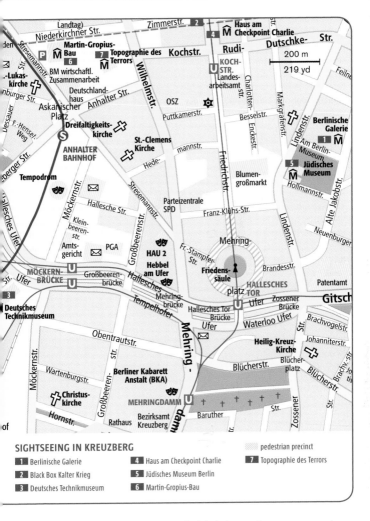

SIGHTSEEING IN KREUZBERG

1 Berlinische Galerie
2 Black Box Kalter Krieg
3 Deutsches Technikmuseum
4 Haus am Checkpoint Charlie
5 Jüdisches Museum Berlin
6 Martin-Gropius-Bau
7 Topographie des Terrors

pedestrian precinct

KREUZBERG

There is a touch of the exotic in the air: the Turkish way-of-life dominates in the north-east of the district in particular – with Turkish cafés (for men only), vegetable shops, markets and bakeries.

And, in between, there are any number of bars, restaurants and clubs for German-Turkish bohemians to let their hair down. Many young people live in the area around Oranienstraße and Oranienplatz – a centre of West Berlin alternative culture while the wall was still standing – and the choice of bars and pubs is correspondingly large.

KREUZBERG

Well-off academics have moved into the chic, renovated factory lofts along the river banks on Fraenkel and Paul-Linke Ufer. A large weekly market is held on Tuesdays and Fridays on the other side of the river, on Maybachufer. The many Turkish stall-holders and their customers create a bazaar-like atmosphere.

1 INSIDER TIP BERLINISCHE GALERIE
(144 B6) (*Ø K5*)

You will be dazzled by the works of the so-called 'Neue Wilden' that evolved around Rainer Fetting, and those of the Expressionists such as Erich Heckel and Ernst Ludwig Kirchner in the State Gallery for Modern Art. New Realism is represented with works by Otto Dix and George Grosz. *Wed–Mon 10am–6pm | entrance fee 6 euros | Alte Jakobstraße 124–28 | www.berlinischegalerie.de | U 1, 6, 15 Hallesches Tor*

2 BLACK BOX KALTER KRIEG
(144 A5) (*Ø K5*)

A 240 square yards big black information box documents the recent German history: starting with the allied victory, followed by the armament and ending with the fall of the communist regime. A map shows the division of Berlin into four sectors by the victorious powers. A real museum to cover this topic is planned here. *Daily 9am–8pm | admission 5 euros | Friedrichstr. 47/ corner of Zimmermann Straße | www.bfgg. de/zentrum-kalter-krieg | U 6 Kochstraße*

3 DEUTSCHES TECHNIKMUSEUM
(151 F2) (*Ø J6*)

Young and old will be delighted by this collection of historical vehicles, instruments and inventions. You will really need more than a day if you want to visit the engine shed with its historic locomotives and the shipping section with 1500 exhibits. The large plane collection in the aviation section is really impressive. *Tue–Fri 9am–5.30pm, Sat/Sun 10am–6pm | entrance fee 6 euros | Trebbiner Str. 9 | www.sdtb. de | U 1, 2 Gleisdreieck*

4 HAUS AM CHECKPOINT CHARLIE
(132 C6) (*Ø K5*)

Permanent exhibition on the construction of the Wall and division of the city. Documentation of attempts to escape and the vehicles used for this: from mini-submarines to hot-air balloons. *Daily 9am until 10pm | entrance 12.50 euros | Friedrichstraße 44 | www.mauermuseum. com | U 6 Kochstraße*

5 JÜDISCHES MUSEUM BERLIN ⭐
(144 B6) (*Ø K5*)

The exhibition in the spectacular building designed by the New York architect Daniel

Not only of great architectural interest: the Jewish Museum

Libeskind that is connected to the old Baroque building shows 2000 years of Jewish culture. Multimedia technology, lighting effects and the unorthodox layout of the exhibition rooms create an emotional connection between the visitors and exhibits.
One of the many subjects dealt with is the history of the persecution of Jews in Germany from the early Middle Ages to the present day. The glass plaza was created by roofing over the former central courtyard. *Mon 10am–10pm, Tue–Sun 10am–8pm | entrance fee 5 euros | Lindenstraße 9–14 | www.jmberlin.de | U 1, 6, 15 Hallesches Tor*

6 MARTIN-GROPIUS-BAU (143 F5) (*J5*)

Originally conceived as a museum for arts and crafts, this magnificent building with its beautiful reliefs and mosaics which was erected between 1877 and 1881 to plans drawn up by Martin Gropius (Walter Gropius' great-uncle) and Heino Schmieden, now serves as an atmospheric location for art and history exhibitions. *Wed–Mon 10am–8pm | varying entrance fees | Niederkirchner Str. 7 | www.gropiusbau.de | S 1, 25 Anhalter Bahnhof*

7 TOPOGRAPHIE DES TERRORS (144 A5) (*J5*)

An open-air exhibition on the site of the former centre of power of the National Socialist, SS police state provides information on the atrocities that were planned and organised here.
There are display boards showing pictures of executed politicians and resistance fighters. A new documentation centre was opened here in 2010. *Daily 10am–8pm | entrance free | guided tours, by appointment | Niederkirchner Straße 8 | www.topographie.de | S 1, 25 Anhalter Bahnhof*

CHARLOTTENBURG/WILMERSDORF

Shopping district, gourmet quarter and an eldorado for culture-vultures – all of this is concentrated in the districts of Charlottenburg between KaDeWe and Schloss Charlottenburg, and Wilmersdorf to the south of Kurfürstendamm.

The number of restaurants around Savignyplatz must break all records, while joggers and museum visitors to the castle park graciously keep out of each other's way. Kurfürstendamm is still the traditional shopping strip for the better-heeled, while the younger crowd gather in the shade of the Memorial Church to hang out together or go bargain-hunting. With the Theater des Westens, Schaubühne, German Opera and Schiller Theatre (the State Opera's temporary home until 2013), Charlottenburg competes with the theatres in the east of the city. Wilmersdorf attracts people with its numerous traditional, speciality shops.

1 FUNKTURM (140 B5) (*C5*)

Modelled on the Eiffel Tower in Paris, but considerably smaller, the Berlin counterpart was erected on the Fair grounds in 1926 and was considered the modern landmark of Berlin for many years. Especially in the divided city the 'beanpole' – as the locals called it – became a symbol for the inhabitants of West Berlin. There is a restaurant 55 m (180 ft) above ground level and a viewing platform 71 m (233 ft) feet higher up. The transmission mast at the top of the tower is used for the police radio. As the tower is often closed for servicing, it is wise to call before you make a visit. *Mon 10am–8pm, Tue–Sun 10am–*

11pm | entrance fee 4.50 euros | tel. 03030 38 19 05 | Charlottenburg | Messedamm | S 7, 41, 42 Messe Nord | U 2 Kaiserdamm

2 KAISER WILHELM GEDÄCHTNIS-KIRCHE (131 E4) (*M G5*)

The bleak ruins of the tower of the church erected between 1891 and 1895 in memory of Kaiser Wilhelm I point into the sky like a warning finger. After it was almost completely destroyed in World War II, church officials decided to at least leave its tower standing. Between 1958 and 1961 a ● modern octagonal church constructed of blue glass bricks, designed by Egon Eiermann, was erected adjacent to it. There is an exhibition on the history of the church on the ground floor of the tower. *Daily 9am until 7pm, Memorial Hall Mon–Sat 10am until 6pm, Sun 12noon–5.30pm, church concert Sat 6pm | Charlottenburg | Breitscheidplatz | www. gedaechtniskirche-berlin.de | U/S Zoologischer Garten*

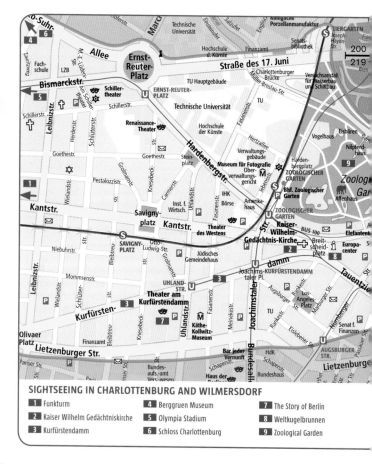

SIGHTSEEING IN CHARLOTTENBURG AND WILMERSDORF

1 Funkturm
2 Kaiser Wilhelm Gedächtniskirche
3 Kurfürstendamm
4 Berggruen Museum
5 Olympia Stadium
6 Schloss Charlottenburg
7 The Story of Berlin
8 Weltkugelbrunnen
9 Zoological Garden

3 KURFÜRSTENDAMM ●
(148–149 C–F 1–2) (*D–F 5–6*)

Before Reunification, this shopping boulevard was the epitome of Berlin's metropolitan flair for the people of West Berlin. Today, you will mainly find Japanese and Russians shopping in the boutiques. Recently, many empty buildings have been demolished and new complexes including the *Kranzlereck*, with offices, shops and a café, have since opened. The boulevard was laid out as a 3.5 km (2 mi) ride between 1883 and 1886 and some houses still bear witness to the opulent turn-of-the-century architecture around 1900. *Charlottenburg | U 1, 9 Kurfürstendamm*

4 BERGGRUEN MUSEUM
(140 C3) (*D4*)

Works by Picasso and Paul Klee form the core of this unique collection assembled by the art dealer Heinz Berggruen. Early works, as well as paintings, sculptures and works on paper, are exhibited under the title 'Picasso and his Time' on three floors in this magnificent building designed by Stüler. *Tue–Sun 10am–6pm | entrance fee 8 euros | Charlottenburg | Schlossstraße 1 | www.smb.museum | S 41, 42 Westend*

Schloss Charlottenburg: Fortuna dancing on the dome

5 OLYMPIA STADIUM
(156 C3) (*A–B4*)

Germany's second largest stadium has space for 75,000 spectators. It was built to plans by the architect Werner March for the 1936 Olympic Games and, today, is mainly used for the games of the Hertha BSC football club. The National Socialist architecture had suffered greatly over the years and the stadium was completely renovated for the 2006 Football World Championship. All seats are now protected from the weather. *Daily 9am–7pm, in winter until 4pm, June–15 Sept 9am–8pm | tours of the stadium daily 11am,* *April–Oct also 1pm, 3pm, June–Aug also 5pm | admission without tour guide 7 euros, including guide 10 euros | Charlottenburg | Olympischer Platz 3 | tel. 030 25 00 23 22 | www.olympiastadion-berlin.de | U 2 Olympiastadion*

SCHLOSS CHARLOTTENBURG ⭐
(140–141 C–D 1–2) (*D4*)

The more than 300-year-old summer residence of the Electress Sophie Charlotte not only impresses with the French-style landscape architecture of its garden with its rows of box trees but, above all, with its grand architecture from the 17th and 18th centuries. The apartments of Friedrich I and his wife are open to the public. The mausoleum of Queen Luise, the wife of Friedrich Wilhelm III, is at the far end of the park. *Old Palace April–Oct Tue–Sun 10am–6pm (Nov–March to 5pm), New Wing April–Oct Wed–Mon 10am–6pm (Nov–March to 5pm),*

Belvedere April–Oct Tue–Sun 10am–6pm (Nov–March 12noon–4pm), Mausoleum April–Oct Tue–Sun 10am–6pm (Nov–March 12noon–5pm), Belvedere (KPM Porcelain Collection), New Pavilion (art and crafts of the Romantic movement) Tue–Sun 10am until 5pm | Charlottenburg | Spandauer Damm | entrance fees Palace 10 euros, New Wing 6 euros, Belvedere, New Pavilion, Mausoleum 3 euros each | www.spsg.de | Bus 145 Luisenplatz

◆6 THE STORY OF BERLIN
(140 C5) (*ฬ F5*)

Going around the 24 rooms will seem like a journey through time during which you will find out a great deal about the history of Berlin. Young people in particular will be fascinated by all the hi-tech and multimedia installations. *Daily 10am–8pm, last admission 6pm | entrance fee 10 euros | Charlottenburg | Kurfürstendamm 207 | www.story-of-berlin.de | U 1 Uhlandstraße*

◆7 WELTKUGELBRUNNEN
(131 E4) (*ฬ G5*)

The Berlin sculptor Joachim Schmettau created this fountain on Breitscheidplatz in 1983. It has since become a popular spot not far from the Memorial Church and Europacenter. Its massiveness led locals to christen it the 'Water Meatball'. However, the granite globe with its arched openings is not particularly clunky at all. Instead, a dazzling spectacle is created by the interaction of flowing water, figures and cascades. *Charlottenburg | Breitscheidplatz | U/S Zoologischer Garten*

◆8 ZOOLOGICAL GARDEN
(131 E–F 3–4) (*ฬ F–G5*)

The 160-year-old zoo is the oldest in Germany and – with its 13,700 animals of 1388 species – the most diverse in the world. Just one highlight: ● the *aquarium* with the crocodile section. *Daily 9am–7pm,* to 5pm in winter | entrance fee 13 euros, with aquarium 20 euros | Charlottenburg | Budapester Straße 5 | www.zoo-berlin.de | U/S Zoologischer Garten*

IN OTHER DISTRICTS

ALLIIERTENMUSEUM
(154 A2–3) (*ฬ C9*)

The subject is the history of the western powers and Berlin in the years from 1945 to 1994. There is an impressive documentation of the Berlin Airlift in 1948/49 and you can even inspect one of the planes the local residents called 'raisin bombers' parked outside. *Thu–Tue 10am–6pm | entrance free | Zehlendorf | Clayallee 135 | www.alliiertenmuseum.de | U 3 Oskar-Helene-Heim*

BOTANISCHER GARTEN ●
(154 C3) (*ฬ E9–10*)

The whole natural world can be found on this 1070-acre site: Siberian steppe grass, Japanese cherry trees and common or garden vegetables located in a spacious park in Stieglitz. Highlights include the huge old buildings housing tropical plants, giant water-lilies, bamboo and palm trees; the orchid hall and cactus collection are also superb. *Daily 9am to nightfall | entrance 6 euros | Stieglitz | entrances Unter den Eichen, Königin-Luise-Straße | www.botanischer-garten-berlin.de | S 1 Botanischer Garten*

BRÜCKE MUSEUM (154 A1) (*ฬ C8*)

This idyllically located single-storey building in Grunewald houses an impressive collection of works by those artists who came together in Dresden in 1905 to form the 'Brücke' (Bridge) group including Ernst Ludwig Kirchner, Erich Heckel, Karl Schmitt-Rottluff, Max Pechstein and

A king-size splash in the hippopotamus house at Berlin Zoo

Emil Nolde. *Wed–Mon 11am–5pm | entrance fee 5 euros | Dahlem | Bussardsteig 9 | www.bruecke-museum.de | bus 115 Pücklerstraße*

INSIDER TIP ▶ GÄRTEN DER WELT
(157 E3) *(꩜ 0)*

Europe's largest Chinese garden, covering an area of 6 ¾ acres, presents a rocky landscape with waterfalls, a lake with bridges, pavilions and many other attractions. Relaxing: the tea ceremony in the ● *Berghaus zum Osmanthussaft (chinese tea ceremony, reservations only, 8 euros | tel. 0179 3 94 55 64).* Included in the grounds are a Japanese garden *(Mon–Fri from 12noon, Sat/Sun from 9am, guided tours Tue–Fri 10.30am–12noon),* an Oriental and a Balinese garden as well as a maze. *Daily from 9am, April–Sept until 8pm, March, Oct until 6pm, Nov–Feb until 4pm, guided tours April–Oct Tue–Fri 11am, 2pm | admission 3 euros, in winter 2 euros| Marzahn | Eisenacher Str. 99 | www.gruen-berlin.de | U 5 Cottbusser Platz, then Bus 195 Erholungspark Marzahn*

GLIENICKER PARK ☆ **(156 B4)** *(꩜ 0)*

A wonderful place to go for a stroll, just as in the days when the prince electors and princesses held hands in the shade of the oak trees and admired the view over the River Havel. Laid out by Lenné and Schinkel at the beginning of the 19th century, the 290-acre English landscaped park is divided into a North-European, an Alpine and a Mediterranean section. The well-tended trees, a Classicist house, Italian pavilions, fountains, pergolas and arcades will make your walk fly by. The round temple with its Corinthian columns that Schinkel designed in 1835 is a real highlight. Spies were exchanged between East and West on Glienicker Bridge at the southern end of the park during the Cold War. *Wannsee | Königstr. | Bus 316 Glienicker Brücke*

GRUNEWALD
(154 A1–2) *(꩜ A–C 5–10)*

When the city was divided by the Wall, Grunewald – the largest wooded area in the western section of the city – was the epitome of a recreation area. Today, it is much more peaceful. Several lakes including *Teufelssee* (Devil's Lake) as well as the River Havel will tempt you to take a swim. Teufelssee is also the site of ☺ *Ökowerk (tel. 030 30 00 50)* which offers a natural garden, beehives and survival courses for children. The 16th century *Jagdschloss Grunewald (April–Oct Tue–Sun 10am–6pm, at other times Sat/Sun 11am–4pm | entrance fee 5 euros)* on the banks of Lake Grunewald has a beautiful Renaissance hall, a valuable collection of paintings and a hunting museum. The 120 m (394 ft) high *Teufelsberg* (Devil's Mountain) in the north was created from the mass of rubble from buildings destroyed during the war. *Grunewald | S 7, 9 Grunewald*

HOUSE OF THE WANNSEE CONFERENCE (156 B4) (*ω 0*)

On 22 January 1942, representatives of the Nazi regime and the SS met in this mansion with a view of the lake to finalise the organisation of the genocide of the Jews based on a decision that had been made previously. An exhibition on the ground floor provides information on the conference, the events leading up to it and its horrific consequences. *Daily 10am–6pm | entrance free | Wannsee | Am Großen Wannsee 56–58 | tel. 030 805 00 10 | www.ghwk.de | S Wannsee, then bus 114 Haus der Wannseekonferenz*

JÜDISCHER FRIEDHOF WEISSENSEE (156 D3) (*ω O–P 1–2*)

More than 115,000 Berlin Jews have found their final resting place here. This makes the cemetery, which was established in 1880, the largest Jewish graveyard in Europe. The brick building and layout of the burial areas were designed by Hugo Licht. A memorial stone has been erected in remembrance of the 6 million Jews who were murdered by the National Socialists. The publishers Samuel Fischer and Rudolf Mosse, as well as the painter Lesser Ury, are among the most prominent people buried here. Men must wear a *kippa* head covering (caps can be borrowed at the entrance). *April–Oct Sun–Thu 8am–5pm, Fri 8am–3pm, Nov–March to 4pm, Fri to 3pm | Weißensee | Herbert-Baum-Str. 45 | tram 12 Albertinenstraße*

PFAUENINSEL ● (156 B4) (*ω 0*)

Originally, the 165-acre Pfaueninsel (Peacock Island) was the site of the zoo that Friedrich Wilhelm III had set up at

FLOATING SWIMMING POOL

Since 2004 the hull of a barge filled with water has been used as a floating swimming pool on the Spree. The water doesn't come from the river but from the tap. The walls of the ship have been lined with blue plastic like any other swimming pool. When it's sunny, the jetties and beach nearby the *Badeschiff* **(146 B5)** (*ω O6*) are bursting with party people. In the evenings, DJs work the turntables. On summer weekends it is often so full that it can take a while before you get a turn to jump into Berlin's biggest bath tub. In winter, the pool is roofed over and combined with a sauna. *May–Sept daily 8am–midnight, in winter 10am–midnight | entrance fee 4 euros, in winter with sauna (3 hrs.) 12 euros, entrance up until 3pm 8 euros | Treptow / Eichenstr. 4 | tel. 030 53 32 03 82 | www.arena-berlin.de | S-Bahn Treptower Park*

Prussian playfulness: the little white castle on Pfaueninsel

the beginning of the 19th century. Today, only the peacocks in the wild and the romantic park are a reminder of the island's original purpose. The little white castle looks like a film set. It was built for Wilhelmine Enke, the paramour of Friedrich Wilhelm II. Take a look at the dairy and the hall in the style of a Gothic Revival church where parties were held. *Wannsee | Pfaueninselchaussee | ferry every day of the year | 3 euros | Castle May–Sept Tue–Thu 10am–6pm, Oct Tue–Sun 10am–5pm; dairy June–Sept Mon–Fri 10am–5pm, Sat/sun 10am–6pm, Oct daily 10am–5pm | entrance fee 3 euros | www.spsg.de | tel. 030 80 58 68 31 | bus 218 Pfaueninsel*

INSIDER TIP RIXDORF
(157 D4) (*M N8*)

This small village with its sheds and forges, once founded by the Bohemians, is situated in the middle of the Neuköllner mass of houses. Here you get a feeling of how the Berlin metropole once grew out of many small locations. Pretty: the Bohemian Bethlehem Church and the Bohemian Cemetery. *U 7 Karl-Marx-Straße*

SOWJETISCHES EHRENMAL
(146 C6) (*M P7*)

One of the largest Soviet military cemeteries in Germany is located in Treptower Park. Not only the grave slabs in memory of the 7000 Soviet soldiers who fell in the Battle of Berlin are impressive, the sheer size of the complex is also astonishing: eight walls with reliefs, the monumental 60 m (40 ft) high bronze sculpture of a soldier carrying a rescued German child, as well as the gigantic sculpture 'Mother Homeland' that was chiselled out of a 50-ton block of granite. The monument was erected between 1947 and 1949. *Treptow | Alt-Treptow 1| S Treptower Park*

INSIDER TIP STASI PRISON HOHENSCHÖNHAUSEN
(157 E3) (*M O2*)

Grey functional buildings, walls and barbed wire give an impression of how

Sowjetisches Ehrenmal in Treptow

TEMPELHOFER PARK
(152 A–C 5–6) (*ψ K–M 7–9*)

Even today Europe's biggest office build-ing, the central building of the Tempel-hof airport, with a length of 1300yd and 5000 rooms, gives an impression of the monumental architecture of the National Socialism. Opened in 1936 for the Olympic Games in Berlin, an inter-national flying hub and the seat for the air ministry was planned. This airport is no longer in use since 2008 and plans are to convert this area into a landscape park until 2017. Currently INSIDER TIP *the airfield is used by joggers, skaters and strollers during the day.*

On *Platz der Luftbrücke* a monument pays homage to the Berin Airlift dur-ing the soviet Berlin blockade 1948/49. Counterparts can be seen at Frank-furt Airport/Main and in Celle. *Guided tours of the building Mon–Fri 4pm, Fri also 1pm, Sat/Sun 11am, 2pm | 12 eu-ros| Tempelhof | Platz der Luftbrücke | www.tempelhoferfreiheit.de | U 6 Platz der Luftbrücke*

TIERPARK FRIEDRICHSFELDE
(157 E3) (*ψ S5–6*)

Enjoy this spacious zoo which houses around 7500 animals of over 800 spe-cies, located in what was once a castle park designed by the famous landscape architect Peter Joseph Lenné. Highlights include the walk-in Vari-Wald (lemurs from Madagascar) and the Malayan bear house. The early-Classicist *Friedrichsfelde Castle (Tue–Sun 10am–6pm)* is open again now that the renovations have been completed; concerts are frequent-ly held in the main hall. *Daily 9am–7pm, to 5pm in winter | entrance fee 12 euros | Lichtenberg | Am Tierpark 125 | www.tierpark-berlin.de | tel. 030 51 53 10 | U 5 Tierpark*

political prisoners were kept in solitary confinement. People who actually expe-rienced this guide you through the build-ing and help you understand what peo-ple had to suffer who were subjected to the psychological torture of the East German secret police. *Guided tours hourly Mon–Fri 11am–3pm, Sat, Sun 10am–4pm | entrance fee 5 euros | Hohenschönhausen | Genselerstraße 66 | tel. 030 98 60 83 30 | www.stiftung-hsh. de | tram 6 Genslerstraße*

EXCURSIONS

KÖPENICK
(157 E4) (*M 0*)

In the German-speaking world, this water-side town to the south-east of Berlin is known due to a story about a bogus captain who confiscated the city's treasury in 1906. Köpenick has been part of Greater Berlin since 1920 but has managed to preserve its own charm. Along with its pretty old town and castle, Müggelsee is the perfect destination for a relaxing day trip away from city life.

The best way to get to Köpenick is on the water. In summer, boats run by the 'Stern und Kreisschifffahrt' *(www.sternundkreis. de)* leave Treptow harbour every hour. The excursion boats take exactly 60 min-

utes to steam upstream along the Spree, past the industrial complexes of former East Germany, the Plänter Forest x and idyllic shoreline properties. Visitors for Köpenick should disembark at Am Luisenhain in the heart of the old town. The famous red-brick *town hall* is directly opposite. In 1906, one year after it was opened, the unemployed shoemaker WilhelmVoigt decided to gain entry into the town hall wearing a captain's uniform, arrest the mayor and steal the borough's coffers. An exhibition in the town hall *(daily 10am–5.30pm | entrance free)* documents the story that inspired the author Carl Zuckmayer to write his famous play 'The Captain of Köpenick'. The events are re-enacted in front of the town hall at 11am on Wednesdays and Saturdays.

KEEP FIT!

The ● *Sultan Hamam* **(151 E2)** *(M H6)* *(daily 12noon–11pm, Tue, Thu–Sat women only, Mon 12noon–11pm men only, Sun family day, | entrance fee for 3 hrs. 16 euros | Schöneberg | Bülowstr. 57 | tel. 030 21 75 33 75 | U 2 Bülowstraße)* is a Turkish-style oriental steam-bath extending over 1000 m² (more than 10,000 square ft). Towels and flip-flops can be hired. Cosmetic treatments. The *Stadtbad Krumme Straße* **(141 E3)** *(M E4)* *(saunas Mon 8am–11pm, Tue–Sun 9am–11pm | ask by phone for opening times of pool | day ticket: saunas 11, pool 4 euros | Charlottenburg | Krumme Str. 10 | tel. 030 34 38 38 60 | U 7 Richard-Wagner-Platz)* is decorated with pretty wall paintings and cast-iron pillars. Sauna area with a bio sauna, Russian-Roman

steam bath and two Finnish saunas. The *Stadtbad Neukölln* **(153 F5)** *(M N8)* *(saunas Tue–Thu 10am–6pm, Fri–Sun 2pm–10pm, Mon 2pm–10pm (women only) | ask by phone for opening times of pool | saunas 14, pool 4 euros | Neukölln | Ganghoferstr. 3 | tel. 030 68 24 98 12 | U 7 Rathaus Neukölln)* with its two pools (built in 1912) is notable for its design based on ancient architecture of bathhouses and its prettily tiled spa area with a steam bath, caldarium, sanarium and herbal sauna. Float in a saltwater tank for that deep, beneficial relaxation. Massages also available in *The Float* **(139 E3)** *(M M1)* *(Thu–Mon 12noon–9pm, in winter daily 12noon–9pm | 35–59 euros | Prenzlauer Berg | Dunckerstraße 12 | tel. 030 44 03 65 00 | Tram 12 Raumerstraße)*.

EXCURSIONS

The magnificent and beautifully restored *Schloss Köpenick*, a moated 17th century castle, is located around 200 metres to the south of the town hall and was originally built for the later King Friedrich I of Prussia. It houses the *Kunstgewerbe-museum (Tue–Sun 10am–6pm | entrance fee 4 euros)* and an exhibition of historical craftsmanship. The castle park, with its delightful café, is an ideal place to take a break with a view of *Frauentog*, a bay on the River Dahme. This is where you can rent a solarboat *(March–Oct 10am–7pm | www.solar-waterworld.de)* for as little as 10 euros an hour and glide silently over the Spree and Dahme. From your boat you will be able to see the *Fischerkietz* (Fisherman's District) – a lovely settlement with historical fishermen's houses and the *Krokodil river beach (May–Sept daily 10am–6pm | entrance fee 3 euros)* – on the eastern shore of the Frauentog.

Excursion boats sail on further from the Luisenhain dock to *Müggelsee*. You can also reach Berlin's largest lake by tram (lines 60 and 61 in the direction of 'Altes Wasserwerk') in around 20 minutes. Get off at the Bölschestraße/Am Wasserwerk stop and walk about 300 m to the lake with its beer garden, beach bar and small – but first-rate – French restaurant *Domaines (www.domaines-berlin.de | Moderate)*. The Spreetunnel leads to the west shore of the lake where there are several places to go swimming. A stroll along the lakeside will take you to the popular, rustic *Rübezahl* inn. During summer, ships depart from here for Friedrichshagen every hour. The quickest way back to the centre of Berlin is then by district line from Freidrichshagen station. *Information: Tourist information Köpenick (Mon–Fri 9am–6.30pm, Sat 10am–4pm, in winter only until 1pm on Saturdays | Alt-Köpenick 31–33 | Am Schlossplatz | tel. 030 65 57 55 01 | www.berlin-tourismus-online.de)*

POTSDAM (156 B4–5) *(Ø 0)*

The capital of Brandenburg attracts many visitors with its chic villas, magnificent castle grounds and Prussian military history. It is located to the south-west of Berlin on the opposite bank of the Havel and can be easily reached on the district line (line 7, every 10 minutes).

Today, what used to be the royal seat of the Prussian kings is a town with a unique cultural and park landscape. Since 1990, large sections of Potsdam have been declared a Unesco World Heritage Site. These include Sanssouci park, the Neuer Garten, Babelsberg and Glienicke (on the Berlin side of the Havel) with their respective castles. ★ *Schloss Sanssouci* park is a magnificent example of French and Italian landscape garden architecture. This is where the tour begins. The *Expressbus X 15 (April–Oct., in winter bus 695)* will take you to the park from Potsdam-Stadt station where the district line from Berlin arrives; get off at the Schloss Sanssouci stop.

Originally, the park was only a terraced garden that Friedrich II (the Great) had laid out in 1744 to cultivate fruit and wine. He then fell in love with the view from the hill to such an extent that he had a palace built above the terraces as his summer residence. The single-storey palace, barely 100 metres long, was constructed by Georg Wenzeslaus von Knobelsdorff in a mere two years (1745–47). Schloss Sanssouci (which means 'without a care') is relatively small and was intended to serve the young king as a place where he could relax. This is where the king spent his summers studying philosophy, music and literature and receiving guests.

Friedrich II had several other buildings, including the *Neue Palais* and the *Chinesisches Teehaus*, erected in addition to the palace. The Neue Palais was the last and, at the same time, largest 18th century construction project in the park at Sanssouci. It

Fruit and wine used to be grown on the terraced gardens at Schloss Sanssouci

was built for Friedrich the Great between 1763 and 1769 to show that he had not been financially ruined by the Silesian wars. A stroll through the park will take you past the Orangery and several other gardens devoted to specific themes.

A 15-minute, signposted, walk from the park exit leads you back to town. The INSIDER TIP *Holländisches Viertel*, erected for Dutch immigrants between 1732 and 1742, is located at Nauener Tor. The soldier-king Friedrich Wilhelm I recruited them as he needed well-trained craftsmen to carry out extensions to his garrison city. Today 'Little Amsterdam' is very popular for its mixture of shops and pubs. The Russian colony Alexandrowka, with 14 small, decorated wooden houses from the early 19th century, is located to the north of the Dutch Quarter. This is where the Russian singers the Tsar had given to King Friedrich Wilhelm II as a present were housed.

Bus 692 from Nauener Tor will take you to *Schloss Cecilienhof (April–Oct. Tue–Sun 10am–6pm, Nov–March Tue–Sun 10am–5pm)* where the Potsdam Conference was held by the Allies in 1945. The palace not only includes an exhibition on the conference but also houses a hotel with a good restaurant *(daily 12noon until 9.30pm | tel. 0331 3 70 50 | Moderate)*. Cecilienhof was constructed between 1914 and 1917 in style of an English country house for Crown Prince Wilhelm and his wife Cecilie; it was the last palace built by the Hohenzollern family.

It is worthwhile making a detour to visit *Krongut Bornstedt (daily 10am–7pm | Ribbeckstr. 6/7 | www.krongut-bornstedt. de)* on the north-west periphery of the town. The former Hohenzollern crown estate and model farm still has a brewery, court bakery and workshops where old techniques are kept alive.

Information*: Potsdam Information (April–Oct Mon–Fri 9.30am–6pm, Sat, Sun 9.30am–4pm, Nov–March Mon–Fri 10am–6pm, Sat, Sun 10am–2pm | Brandenburger Straße 3 | Potsdam | tel. 0331 27 55 80 | www.potsdam.de)*

FOOD & DRINK

Berlin is a gourmet's paradise. There is a wide choice of places to eat ranging from internationally acclaimed restaurants with Michelin stars to excellent Turkish and Russian cuisine.

Alpine cuisine – with all the classics such as Wiener schnitzel, boiled beef and potato salad – is especially popular on the banks of the Spree. There, you can even eat lying down! If you want to eat well without ruining your holiday budget, do this at lunchtime when some of the gourmet restaurants offer attractive set meals at relatively inexpensive prices.But, you will also find local food at acceptable prices in Berlin. Both locals and visitors like substantial meals with fresh ingredients from the area. Nourishing soups are also popular and the many soup bars in the city centre, which offer new dishes every day, are time-honoured institutions. The large number of Italian restaurants also provides a good choice for a quick meal. Interestingly, many are owned by Turks and you will hardly hear a word of Italian coming out of the kitchen. But, in most cases the pizzas and pasta are up to standard and there might only be some discussion about the salads; uninteresting glasshouse produce and ready-made dressings are unfortunately wide-spread. Seeing that Berlin has around 160,000 Turkish residents, there are surprisingly few Turkish restaurants. However, you can find a döner kebab stand on most corners. Most

Photo: Restaurant Margaux

A city of gourmet restaurants and snack bars: everything from currywurst to sushi – Berlin caters to all culinary tastes

people are not aware that pita bread filled with meat and salad is just as much a Berlin invention as currywurst. And then there are the Russians – not only in the form of their own clubs and bars but also their culinary culture. *Beef stroganoff*, *borscht* and *pelmeni* taste especially good washed down with vodka. Asian cooking is still popular although many Chinese restaurants don't come anywhere near the quality of those in their original country. On the other hand,

modern Asian cooking with lemon-grass soup and paeng chicken has many admirers especially now that many restaurant owners have moved away from the kitschy pseudo-Asian interior decoration of former days. Many restaurateurs have managed to remain successful by switching to pan-Asian cooking: Asian dishes with an American or European touch. Eating is always a matter of what is in fashion – especially in a big city like Berlin.

CAFÉS & BREAKFAST

Viennese coffee house with style and tradition: Café Einstein

CAFÉS & BREAKFAST

BONIFAZIUS (153 E3) (*M6*)
Cosy antiques café with a blazing logs in the fireplace and a huge stock of retro-lamps and grandma's furniture. You can even buy the chair you sit on. *Mon–Fri 12noon–8pm, Sat 11am–5pm | Neukölln | Bürknerstr. 26 | U 8 Schönleinstraße*

CAFÉ EINSTEIN ★ (151 D1) (*H5*)
Traditional Viennese-style coffee house in the former villa of the silent-film star Henny Porten. The café of the same name in Mitte *(Unter den Linden 42)* is more modern. Both addresses have some things in common; many prominent regulars, as well as a good menu with boiled beef and excellent cakes. *Daily from 9am | Tiergarten | Kurfürsten-straße 58 | tel. 030 2 61 50 96 | www.cafe einstein.com | U 1 Kurfürstenstraße*

INSIDER TIP ▶ CAFE FREISTIL
(155 E3) (*F9*)
Today, the scent of coffee is in the air at the former Steglitz Baths and the swim-mers have been replaced by guests read-ing newspaper sitting on cushions on tiled benches. Concerts, theatre perfor-mances and readings are also held here. *Daily | Steglitz | Bergstr. 90 | tel. 030 79 74 80 28 | www.stadtbad-steglitz.de | S 1 Feuerbachstraße*

CAFÉ LIEBLING (139 D3) (*M1–2*)
Cosy café on Helmholtzplatz with news-papers and exotic warm drinks made with fresh ingredients including orange, gin-ger and mint tea. First-rate selection of cakes and soups at lunch. *Daily from 9am, Sat/Sun from 10am | Prenzlauer Berg | Raumerstr. 36a | corner of Dunckerstraße | tel. 030 41 19 82 09 | tram 12 Raumer Straße*

CAFÉ IM LITERATURHAUS
(131 D5) (*F5*)
After a stroll down Kurfürstendamm: Coffee, cakes and freshly-made dishes will get you going again. *Daily from 9.30am | Charlottenburg | Fasanenstraße 23 | tel. 030 8 82 54 14 | U1 Uhlandstraße*

DACHGARTENRESTAURANT KÄFER IM DEUTSCHEN BUNDESTAG ❄️
(132 A3) (𝄞 J4)

The only parliament that is daring enough to have a restaurant on its roof – and that with a fantastic view and the quality Käfer is famous for. Here, you can feast to your heart's content. In summer, the terrace is also open. *Daily 9am–4.30pm and 6.30pm–midnight, breakfast 9am–10am | Mitte | Platz der Republik | tel. 030 226 29 90 | www.feinkost-kaefer.de | U/S Friedrichstraße*

FUSSBAD CAFÉ ●
(138 C5) (𝄞 L2)

A cosmetic studio that is also a café: while your feet soak in a bath with flowers and essences, you can relax with a cup of tea or coffee in cosy surroundings. A 20-minute footbath, including coffee and cake, costs 17 euros (reservation necessary). *Mon–Fri 10am–8pm, Sat/Sun 10am–6pm | Mitte | Zionskirchstraße 32 | tel. 030 4 97 87 37 99 | www.fussbadcafe. de | U 8 Bernauer Straße*

MANOLO (139 D4) (𝄞 L2)

Observe what's going on at one of the busiest junctions in town over a caffè latte and a cake or fruit salad – pure big-town bliss! The fine selection of newspapers and comfortable leather benches also will help you feel at home in this self-service café. If your German is up to it, you can play stories by Berlin authors on the CD player. *Daily from 7am | Prenzlauer Berg | Schönhauser Allee 45/corner of Danziger Straße | tel. 030 24 62 79 58 | U 2 Eberswalder Straße*

MEIN HAUS AM SEE ● (138 B5) (𝄞 K3)

This is the place to drink your first – or last – cappuccino at 4 o'clock in the morning. Welcoming design with many sofas and chairs, and street art on the walls. *Daily open 24 hours | Mitte | Brunnenstraße 197–98 | tel. 030 23 88 35 61 | www-mein-haus-am-see.blogspot.com | U 6 Rosenthaler Platz*

OXYMORON (133 E2) (𝄞 L3)

Lovely café-restaurant with Jugendstil charm in the Hackesche Höfe; large selection of breakfast dishes, high-quality Mediterranean cuisine at lunch and, in the evening, good wine and cocktail selection. *Daily from 8am | Mitte |*

MARCO POLO HIGHLIGHTS

⭐ **Café Einstein Tiergarten**
Outstanding coffee, polite service and cosy Viennese coffeehouse charm → p. 66

⭐ **Fischers Fritz**
Haute cuisine in the hotel's kitchen – not only for fish fans → p. 68

⭐ **Margaux**
The chef spoils you with dishes with a touch of France → p. 68

⭐ **Clärchens Ballhaus**
In the most beautiful courtyard garden of the city centre you can eat organic meatballs or pizzas served by efficient waiters → p. 69

⭐ **Horváth**
Gourmet cuisine of a different kind: unpretentious ambience with a flair in the heart of the Kreuzberger Kiez → p. 71

⭐ **Sage Restaurant**
Rough industrial surroundings, white tablecloths → p. 73

Rosenthaler Straße 40–41 | tel. 030 28 39 18 86 | www.oxymoron-berlin. de | S Hackescher Markt

PRINCESS CHEESECAKE ☺
(134 B8) (*ⓜ L3*)

Magnificent cakes made with organic ingredients with an emphasis on its namesake. Cheesecake sounds despicable, the aim here is to reach for higher goals and the results taste damn good! *Daily*

12noon–7pm | Mitte | Tucholskystr. 37 | tel. 030 28 09 27 60 | S 1, 2, 25 Oranienburger Straße

SANKT OBERHOLZ (138 C5) (*ⓜ L3*)

Popular, 'in' café with wifi connection and tennis-umpire chairs in front of the entrance. Sitting up there, guests have a fine view of one of the liveliest junctions in the city where Rosenthalerstraße, Brunnenstraße and Torstraße meet. It's

GOURMET RESTAURANTS

Facil (132 A6) (*ⓜ K4*)

Enjoy this open air restaurant with specialities such as Loup de Mer and Bread salad with quails on the 5th floor of the *Mandala-Hotel*. In summer the glass roof of this gourmet temple is simply slid back. Menus 45–100 euros. *Sat, Sun closed | Tiergarten | Potsdamer Str. 3 | tel. 030 590 05 12 34 | www.facil.de | U/S Potsdamer Platz*

Fischers Fritz ★ (132 C4) (*ⓜ K4*)

Among the dishes the 2-star chef Christian Lohse pampers his guests with in the sophisticated surroundings of the The Regent Hotel Berlin are slice of turbot with saffron-crustacean jus and Provençal potato purée. There is a three-course set lunch for 49 euros. *Daily | Mitte | Charlottenstr. 49 | tel. 030 20 33 63 63 | www.fischersfritz berlin.de | U 6 Französische Straße*

Margaux ★ (132 B4) (*ⓜ J4*)

Château Margaux was the inspiration behind this gourmet temple with its gold-leaf decoration in a premium location. His specialities with their French flavour have led to the chef

Michael Hoffman regularly being awarded a Michelin star. Exclusive wines. Main dishes around 40 euros. *Only evenings, Sunday closed | Mitte | Unter den Linden 78 | tel. 030 22 65 26 11 | www.margaux-berlin. de | S 1 Brandenburger Tor*

Restaurant Tim Raue (144 B5) (*ⓜ K5*)

The famous TV and Michelin-star cook and his wife opened their own restaurant in Kreuzberg in 2010. His cooking is inspired by Asia – at the very highest level. Pork chin, shimeji mushrooms and king crab should bring him his second Michelin star. Set meal (6 courses) from 148 euros. *Mon closed | Kreuzberg | Rudi-Dutschke-Straße 26 | tel. 030 25 93 79 30 | www. tim-raue.com | U 6 Kochstraße*

Vau (133 D4) (*ⓜ K4*)

The unpretentious atmosphere with Thonet chairs and modern art is perfectly suited to Kolja Kleeberg's masterfully plain menu policy. Main dishes from around 40 euros. *Sun closed | Mitte | Jägerstr. 54/55 | tel. 030 20 02 97 30 | www. vau-berlin.de | U 6 Französische Straße*

quieter inside; good selection of coffee specialities. *Daily | Mitte | Rosenthaler Str. 72a | tel. 030 24 08 55 86 | www. sanktoberholz.de | U 8 Rosenthaler Platz*

THEODOR TUCHER (132 B4) (*Ø J4*)

Guests who are interested in literature can relax in comfortable chairs and browse through the latest books on the gallery of this literary café near Brandenburg Gate. If all this reading makes you hungry, good German food is served one floor below. *Daily from 7am | Mitte | Pariser Platz 6a | tel. 030 22 48 94 64 | www.theodortucher. de | S 1 Brandenburger Tor*

GARDEN RESTAURANTS

CLÄRCHENS BALLHAUS ⭐
(138 B6) (*Ø K3*)

Its courtyard garden is especially attractive in summer. Organic meatballs, pizza and cakes served with a flourish. *Daily from 10am | Mitte | Auguststr. 24 | tel. 030 282 92 95 | www.ballhaus.de | S Oranienburger Straße | Budget*

INSIDER TIP DECKSHAUS
(145 D4) (*Ø L4*)

You sit on the deck of the tug 'Jesinky' in the historical harbour and eat sprats, meatballs and fish specialities. A great place to have a beer and listen to the Spree flowing by. *Closed on Mondays in winter | Mitte | Märkisches Ufer 1z | tel. 0174 8 71 51 07 | www.deckshaus.de | U 2 Märkisches Museum | Budget*

FREISCHWIMMER (146 B5) (*Ø O6*)

Idyllic location on the banks of a so-called 'flood channel'. Creative summer cuisine. Young crowd. INSIDER TIP Canoes and kayaks can be hired! *Mon–Fri from 12noon, Sat/Sun from 10am | Kreuzberg | Vor dem Schlesischen Tor 2a | tel. 030 61 07 43 09 |*

VAU, a star in the gourmet firmament

www.freischwimmer-berlin.de | U 1 Schlesisches Tor | Budget

SCHOENBRUNN (139 E6) (*Ø N3*)

Families and the 'in' crowd from 'Prenzel-berg' enjoy their pizza, pasta and anti-pasti in the Friedrichshain Volkspark. Perfect after (or before) a stroll through the park. Large beer garden. *Daily | Friedrichshain | Am Schwanenteich 1 | tel. 030 453 05 65 25 | www.schoenbrunn. net | tram 10 Kniprodestraße/corner of Danziger Str. | Budget*

Chef Loriano Mura gives the finishing touches to a dish in the Bocca di Bacco

THE CLASSICS

HENNE (145 D5) (*M5*)

A true classic when it comes to **INSIDER TIP** crispy chicken. Families, students, intellectuals and long-time residents nibble chicken legs and sip their beer in this unsophisticated hostelry. It is often full and you might have to wait. *Only evenings, closed on Monday | Kreuzberg | Leuschnerdamm 25 | tel. 030 6 14 77 30 | www.henne-berlin.de | U 8, 15 Kottbusser Tor | Budget*

PRATER (138 C4) (*L2*)

The traditional place for raising your tankard and enjoying good food from the grill. On sunny days, families and students bring their picnics with them and enjoy the large beer garden. *Daily from 12noon; in winter, only in the evening | Prenzlauer Berg | Kastanienallee 7–9 | tel. 030 448 56 88 | www.pratergarten.de | U 2 Eberswalder Straße | Budget–Moderate*

WELTRESTAURANT MARKTHALLE (153 E–F1) (*M5*)

The right address for Sauerbraten, goulash and co. Unpretentious classics for those who still remember the student protests of '68 and their successors. *Daily from 10am | Kreuzberg | Pücklerstr. 34 | tel. 030 617 55 02 | www.weltrestaurant-markthalle.de | U 1, 15 Görlitzer Bahnhof | Budget–Moderate*

ZUR LETZTEN INSTANZ (145 D3) (*L4*)

One of the founding fathers of Berlin's cooking culture. The names of the dishes such as 'cross-examination' and 'lawyer's breakfast' remind you that the homey pub is not far away from the law court. *Closed Sunday | Mitte | Waisenstraße 14–16 | tel. 030 2 42 55 28 | www.zurletzteninstanz.de | U 2 Klosterstraße | Budget–Moderate*

RESTAURANTS: EXPENSIVE

BOCCA DI BACCO (132 C4) (*K4*)

Ravioli with loup de mer in shrimp cream, octopus carpaccio and lamb with a herb crust appeal to business people, politicians and gourmets alike. Good wine list. The wine cellar, with a long wooden table for 20 guests, is especially atmospheric (more than 500 wines from Italy alone!). Reservations essential. *Mon–Sat from*

12noon, Sun from 6pm | Mitte | Friedrichstr. 167/168 | tel. 030 20 67 28 28 | www.boc-cadibacco.de | U 6 Französische Straße

HORVÁTH ★ (147 D–E2) *(ⁿ M6)*

Not especially elegant, but the ingredients and compositions are truly splendid. The chef Sebastian Frank considers quality more important than white tablecloths. No matter whether it is slice of halibut on pumpkin purée or fillet of beef on a ragout of root vegetables in red-wine sauce, you will really savour the cuisine in this restaurant, whose chef holds one Michelin star. *Tue–Sun from 6pm | Kreuzberg | Paul-Lincke-Ufer 44a | tel. 030 61 28 99 92 | www.restaurant-horvath.de | U 1, 8 Kottbusser Tor*

LOCHNER (142 C5) *(ⁿ H5)*

The unassuming interior harmonises with the reduced gourmet cuisine. The rack of lamb with red-wine shallots and leek and herb crêpes is pure poetry, as is the monkfish with ox-cheek ravioli and spinach. The accompanying wines are just as convincing. *Tue–Sun from 6pm | Tiergarten | Lützowplatz 5 | tel. 030 23 00 52 20 | www.lochner-restaurant.de | U 1, 15 Nollendorfplatz*

PARIS-MOSKAU (143 D2) *(ⁿ H3)*

The home-style gourmet cooking – such as Havel pike-perch on 'heaven and earth' and fried black pudding – tastes particularly good in this small, half-timbered building next to the railway tracks that has managed to survive the remodelling of the government district. *Daily; Sat, Sun, only in the evening | Tiergarten | Alt-Moabit 141 | tel. 030 3 94 20 81 | www.paris-moskau.de | S Hauptbahnhof*

RESTAURANTS: MODERATE

AIGNER (132 C4) *(ⁿ K4)*

Refined German and Austrian cuisine in classical surroundings: Sauvignon blanc is served with the Palatine 'winegrower's salad' and this is followed by black-pudding dumplings on Riesling cabbage accompanied by a Horcher cuvée from Aigner's own vineyards. *Daily from 12noon | Mitte | Französische Str. 25 | tel. 030 2 03 75 18 50 | www-aigner-gendarmenmarkt.de | U 2 Französische Straße*

BANDOL SUR MER (144 B1) *(ⁿ K3)*

French restaurant with country-style cooking: the dishes include stewed beef with black salsify, and loup de mer. Next door there's the lure of the owners new bistro. *Daily from 6pm | Mitte | Torstraße 167 | Tel. 030 67 30 20 51 | U 8 Rosenthaler Platz*

INSIDER TIP ▶ BIEBERBAU
(150 A–B5) *(ⁿ G7)*

The dishes get their characteristic touch from a refined amalgamation of German cooking with a touch of the Mediterranean. Pickled knuckle of pork with truffles, pike-perch with taglierini and Maître Philippe's fine selection of cheese to finish with. Delicious. *Daily from 6pm | Wilmersdorf | Durlacher Straße 15 | tel. 030 8 53 23 90 | www.bieberbau-berlin.de | U/S Bundesplatz*

DOMKLAUSE (133 E3) *(ⁿ L4)*

East German-style restaurant with specialities Honecker and the boys liked to eat. The chef Hans-Jürgen Leucht, the former sous-chef in the old Domklause, makes sure everything is authentic. *Daily from 10am | Mitte | Karl-Liebknecht-Str. 1 | tel. 030 847 12 37 37 | www.ddr-restaurant.de | S Hackescher Markt*

ENGELBECKEN ☺ (140 C5) *(ⁿ D5)*

Seasonal, alpine cuisine in Berlin, on the lakeside at Lietzensee, homey and substantial: Weißwurst, roast pork with dumplings and red cabbage, meat loaf with mustard and pretzels, gnocchi with sage butter for those who have something

LOCAL SPECIALITIES

▶ **Berliner Weiße** – With a shot, a typical drink for the ladies that the lords of creation regard with disdain. Whoever would pour woodruff or raspberry syrup into wheat beer? Women in Berlin like it.

▶ **Buletten** – Almost every butcher has these meatballs ready to be eaten (photo right) and they are also sold at snack bars as curry-buletten. The word comes from the Huguenots; in French, 'boulette' means little ball.

▶ **Currywurst** – Bratwurst with ketchup and curry (photo left) is sold on most street corners in Berlin. The snack-bar owner, Herta Heuwer, came up with the recipe more than 50 years ago.

▶ **Döner kebab** – Pita bread filled with grilled veal and salad. A speciality that is just as much at home in Berlin as the currywurst.

▶ **Eisbein** – Pickled knuckle of pork served with puréed peas. You will need at least one schnapps to go with it...

▶ **Kasseler** – Smoked rib of pork that does not come from the town of Kassel: a Berlin butcher of the same name is responsible for its fame. A decent serving of sauerkraut to go along with it is almost obligatory.

▶ **Quark mit Leinöl** – Curd cheese with linseed oil is regularly eaten in many Berlin households. The cheese is mixed with the oil and a pinch of salt and served with boiled potatoes – simple, but delicious!

▶ **Schmalzstulle** – Pieces of bread with various spreads (Stullen) are once again becoming popular; best of all, hearty and in this case spread with pork dripping and a pinch of salt. Good luck!

▶ **Chocolate** – Those with a sweet-tooth should try some Berlin chocolate. Haman, as well as Fassbender & Rauch, produce first rate quality – and have done so for decades.

against meat, and delicious cakes are tremendously popular. The meat comes from animals that were kept in a humane manner. *Daily; Mon–Sat, only in the evening | Charlottenburg | Witzlebenstraße 31 | tel. 030 6 15 28 10 | www.engelbecken.de | U 2 Sophie-Charlotte-Platz*

ENTRECÔTE (144 B5) (*M K5*)
This is the address for steak fans. French specialities from Angus beef, as well as calf's kidneys in Madeira sauce, in charming surroundings with high ceilings and friendly service. *Daily; Sat, Sun, only in the evening | Mitte | Schützenstr. 5 | tel.*

030 20 16 54 96 | www.entrecote.de | U 2, 6 Stadtmitte

HOSTARIA DEL MONTE CROCE
(152 B3) (*M K6*)

Italy in the building at the back: the feast begins every evening at 7.30; the cooking is just like it is in Emilia Romagna. The guests sit at long tables and all enjoy the same nine-course meal. It changes every four weeks. The wine comes straight from the barrel and you can drink as much as you want. Reservation essential. *Tue–Sat from 7.30pm | Kreuzberg | Mittenwalder Str. 6 | tel. 030 6 94 39 68 | www.hostaria. de | U 7 Gneisenaustraße*

LUTTNER & WEGNER IM WEINHAUS HUTH (143 F5) (*M J5*)

Wiener schnitzel and sauerbraten are the most popular dishes with the regulars in this small restaurant-cum-wine shop. And, all that in the oldest house on Potsdamer Platz. *Daily from 11am | Tiergarten | Alte Potsdamer Str. 5 | tel. 030 25 29 75 24 | U/S Potsdamer Platz*

NOCTI VAGUS (145 D1) (*M M3*)

Dark restaurant with a show programme to tickle the palate: as your eyes give up their function, your senses of taste and smell increase. The chef leads the guests down new aromatic paths: rabbit in plum-wine sauce or strawberries with green pepper. *Daily from 6pm | Mitte | Saarbrücker Straße 36–38 | tel. 030 74 74 91 23 | www.noctivagus.de | U 2 Senefelderplatz*

RIO GRANDE ☙ (146 A4) (*M N5*)

The 'big river' here is the Spree: you can enjoy your creamy veal goulash with buttered gnocchi, fried chicken with potato salad and fresh apple strudel with a wonderful view across the water from the beautiful terrace. *Mon–Fri 11.30am–mid-night, Sat/Sun 10am–midnight | Kreuzberg | May-Ayim-Ufer 9 | tel. 030 61 07 49 81 | www. riogrande-berlin.de | U1 Schlesisches Tor*

SAGE RESTAURANT ★
(145 F5) (*M N5*)

This is where industrial architecture meets pizza and fresh brook char: the restaurant landscape in this gigantic brick building on the Spree varies from sophisticated cuisine to home-style cooking. Lovely lounge with a fireplace for smokers. *Daily; Oct–April only in the evening and Sun from 11am | Kreuzberg | Köpenicker Str. 18–20 | tel. 030 755 49 40 71 | www.sage-restaurant.de | U1 Schlesisches Tor*

SARAH WIENER IM HAMBURGER BAHNHOF (143 E–F1) (*M J3*)

Cuisine from the alpine countries is served in a side wing of the Hamburger Bahnhof Museum. Beautiful terrace on the bank of

The chef recommends...

the Nordkanal. Other locations: *Chaussee-straße 8 (Mitte)* and in the *Museum für Kommunikation* the *Kaffeehaus (Mitte | Leipziger Str. 16)*. Mon–Fri 12noon–4pm and 6pm–11pm, Sat 6pm–11pm | Mitte | Invalidenstr. 50–51 | tel. 030 70 71 36 50 | www.sarahwiener.de | U/S Hauptbahnhof

SCHNEEWEISS
(146 C3) (*∅ O5*)

The name Snow White is the restaurant's motto – the only colour here is on the plates. The Wiener schnitzel has a golden

---

LOW BUDGET

▶ The pizza-like slices (1.50 euros each) with their wonderful toppings sold by the *Focacceria* will fill you up in next to no time. **(138 C5)** (*∅ L2*) (daily from 11am | Mitte | Fehrbelliner Str. 24 | tel. 030 44 03 27 71 | U 8 Rosenthaler Platz)

▶ *Schmuck's Restauration*, located at Märkisches Museum, offers the best roasted chicken, but also ,Tafel-spitz' and curd cheese strudel at rea-sonable prices **(145 D4)** (*∅ L4–5*) (Mon–Fri 11.30am–2.30pm | Mitte | Am Köllnischen Park 1 | tel. 030 22 33 65 17 | U 8 Heinrich-Heine-Straße)

▶ ● *Curry 36* **(152 A3)** (*∅ K6*) (Kreuzberg | Mehringdamm 36 | U 6, 7 Mehringdamm) is probably the most popular snack bar in Kreuzberg and not only serves currywurst (around 1.50 euros) with chips but also pea soup (2.50 euros). You eat standing up – and that, right through until the early hours of the morning.

---

smile for the guests and the goat's cheese points southwards. *Daily from 8am | Friedrichshain | Simplonstr. 16 | tel. 030 29 04 97 04 | www.schneeweiss-berlin.de | U/S Warschauer Straße*

UMSPANNWERK OST
(146 A2) (*∅ N4*)

Once electricity flowed here but today wine, cocktails and beer are poured into glasses. This, along with gnocchi and Wiener schnitzel. Huge hall with 7-m-high ceiling and open kitchen. The INSIDER TIP dinner shows are fun! *Daily from 11.30am | Friedrichshain | Palisadenstr. 48 | tel. 030 42 80 94 97 | www.umspannwerk-ost.de | U 5 Weberwiese*

RESTAURANTS: BUDGET

BABA ANGORA (141 F5) (*∅ F5*)

First-rate Turkish cuisine with quality lamb dishes, grilled vegetables and seductive desserts. Homey atmosphere, reasonably-priced set meals at lunchtime. *Mon–Fri from 12noon | Charlottenburg | Schlüterstraße 29 | tel. 030 3 23 70 96 | www.babaangora.de | S Savignyplatz*

GASTHAUS LENTZ
(141 D5) (*∅ E5*)

A classic that not only attracts the old student crowd from '68 who live in the neighbouring flats. Kölsch beer is served, there is no music to disturb your conversa-tion, and there is a variety of lunchtime specials. Meatballs and Landjäger sau-sages are always available. *Daily from 9am | Charlottenburg | Stuttgarter Platz 20 | tel. 030 3 24 16 19 | www.gasthaus-lentz-berlin.de | S Charlottenburg*

GNADENBROT (150 C2) (*∅ G6*)

Goulash, roasts and baked potatoes: that is the recipe of this pub in the centre of town. Its proximity to the gay scene in

Schöneberg is instantly noticeable. It is like a trip back to the 1970s with self-service, checked tablecloths and toothpicks on the tables. *Daily from 3pm | Schöneberg | Martin-Luther-Str. 20a/corner of Motzstr. | tel. 030 21 96 17 86 | www.raststaette-gnadenbrot.de | U 4 Victoria-Luise-Platz*

KIMCHI PRINCESS (153 E2) (*Ø M6*)

'In' restaurant in Kreuzberg with Korean dishes prepared on a cast-iron barbeque at your table. Creative restaurant design with a red metal wall and wooden tables. *Tue–Sun from 6pm | Kreuzberg | Skalitzer Str. 36 | tel. 0163 4 58 02 03 | www.kim chiprincess | U 1 Görlitzer Bahnhof*

INSIDER TIP MERCAN
(153 E2) (*Ø M6*)

Turkish home-style cooking in a simple but friendly atmosphere: the white beans, grilled vegetables, lamb dishes and meatballs are very popular as is the Turkish rice pudding. *Daily | Kreuzberg | Wiener Str. 10 | tel. 030 61 28 58 41 | U 1 Görlitzer Bahnhof*

INSIDER TIP NÖ! WEINGALERIE
(144 A4) (*Ø K4*)

Small, first-class wine shop with a homey atmosphere and wine-tasting. For 15 euros, guests can choose five wines to wash down the cheese and baguette that accompany them. *Mon–Fri from 12noon, Sat from 7pm | Mitte | Glinkastr. 23 | tel. 030 2 01 08 71 | www.cafe-noe.de | U 2, 6 Stadtmitte*

SASAYA (139 D3) (*Ø M1*)

Laid-back service; good, reasonably priced food. The quality of the raw-fish dishes even draws in Japanese guests. *Thu–Mon from 12noon | Prenzlauer Berg | Lychener Str. 50 | tel. 030 44 71 77 21 | U 2 Eberswalder Straße*

TARTANE (132 C1) (*Ø K3*

Even without the impressive tiled mosaics that look different from every angle,

Good and reasonably-priced: La Focacceria in Mitte

the burgers, chicken-wings in cola with salad and roast-beef potatoes à la Yucatan would still make a visit worthwhile. *Daily from 6pm | Mitte | Torstraße 225 | tel. 030 44 72 70 36 | U6 Oranienburger Tor*

INSIDER TIP TOCA ROUGE
(132 C1) (*Ø K3*)

Over-the-top setting in black with an artistically abstract Mao over the entrance. The food is a interesting mixture from all over Asia; pike-perch comes disguised as 'A Better tomorrow'. 'Seven seconds' – roast beef with cucumbers, mushrooms and mustard sauce – is delicious. *Daily, Sat/Sun only evenings | Mitte | Torstraße 195 | tel. 030 84 71 21 42 | S1, Oranienburger Straße*

SHOPPING

CITY **WHERE TO START?**

Alexa on Alexanderplatz and **Tauentzienstraße** near the Gedächt-niskirche will be the first choice for fans of today's fast-selling fashion labels. This is also the home of the **KaDeWe** (Department Store of the West), that is so steeped in tradition. Those who are more interested in small boutiques with clothes by Berlin designers will find what they are looking for in the **Hackesche Höfe** and on **Alte** and **Neue Schönhauser Straße**. **Bergmannstraße** is the place for second-hand articles.

Berlin has so many good shopping streets that it is impossible to list them all. And, if you are looking for the real shopping heart of the city, you won't really be able to pin-point it. There is a simple reason for this: there excellent shopping areas in almost every district.

In Mitte, this is Friedrichstraße with its exclusive boutiques. The clientele in the *Galeries Lafayette* and *Quartier 206* is just as international as the brand names. On the other hand, Germany's largest Kaufhof department store and the *Alexa shopping centre* attract shoppers to Alexanderplatz. Kurfürstendamm, with its many designer boutiques, and Tauentzienstraße with *Peek & Cloppenburg*, *Wertheim* and *KaDeWe*

Photo: Quartier 206

Shopping areas and arcades are not just concentrated on the centre – each district has its own shopping centres and specialist shops

department stores are the pride and joy of Charlottenburg's retail world. In Zehlendorf and Steglitz people stroll along Schlossstraße. And, then there are all the resourceful shop-owners in smaller streets such as Goltzstraße in Schöneberg – well-known for its fashion boutiques. Reuterstraße in Neukölln is an eldorado if you are looking for second-hand things. The area around the Hackesche Höfe is renowned for its fashion and design outlets.

BERLINER ANTIKMARKT
(132 C3) (*ØJ K4*)

Thirty-five antique dealers offer old dolls, toys, watches, clocks, jewellery and paintings in the arches at Friedrichstraße Station. *Bärenstark* has some fine period pieces. *Closed Tue | Mitte | Georgenstraße/S-Bahn-Bögen 190–203 | http://www.berliner-antikmarkt.de|U/S Friedrichstraße*

Sweet delicacies from Istanbul in the Confiserie Orientale

DÜWAL (130 B4) (ﾑ F5)

Lovers of old books treasure those on offer at this renowned shop. The valuable tomes are stacked to the ceiling. *Mo–Fri 3pm–6pm, Sat 11am–2pm | Charlottenburg | Schlüterstraße 17 | www.duewal.de | S Savignyplatz*

INSIDER TIP PLATTEN PEDRO
(135 D6) (ﾑ D–E3)

Berlin's largest source of old records with around 200,000 singles. The demanding collector will find everything from folk music to hard rock to make his heart beat faster. *Mon–Fri 10am–6pm, Sat 10am–2pm | Charlottenburg | Tegeler Weg 102 | www.platten-pedro.de | U 7 Mierendorffplatz*

BEAUTY

NIVEA HOUSE (132 C4) (ﾑ K4)

Enormous selection of cosmetics. You can have a quick restoration session in the beauty salon. A facial (20 minutes including a drink) costs 19 euros. If you are tense, a neck-and-shoulder massage will loosen you up. *Mitte | Unter den Linden 28 | www.nivea.de, link: Nivea Haus Berlin | U/S Brandenburger Tor*

THE ENGLISH SCENT
(130 B3) (ﾑ E–F5)

Famous for its somewhat eccentric British perfumes that cannot be found in any other shops in Berlin. Most of the scents come from purveyors by appointment to Her Majesty the Queen. You will receive expert advice if you are not sure which perfume suits you best. *Mon, Tue, Thu, Fri 10am–2pm and 3–6.30pm, Wed from 2pm, Sat 10am–3pm | Charlottenburg | Goethestraße 15 | www.english-scent.de | S Savignyplatz*

DELIKATESSEN

INSIDER TIP CONFISERIE ORIENTALE
(144 B1) (ﾑ K3)

One of Istanbul's best confectioners produces exclusively for this small shop which offers any amount of marzipan and nougat sweets and all sorts of exotic flavours. Try some yourself over a cup of Mokka in the shop and then take some home with you all packed up beautifully in little boxes. *Tue–Fri 11am–7pm, Sat 12noon–6pm | Mitte | Linienstraße 26 | www.confiserie-orientale. de | S1, 2, 25 Oranienburger Straße*

FRESH 'N' FRIENDS ☺ (132 C1) (*𝄞 L2*)

The organic food shop Fresh'n'Friends is open around the clock and you will have no trouble buying vanilla-flavoured soya milk or banana beer at three in the morning. There is also a branch at Kastanienalle 26 (Prenzlauer Berg). *Open 24 hours a day | Mitte | Friedrichstraße 120 | www.freshn friends.com | U6 Oranienburger Tor*

GOLDHAHN & SAMPSON (139 D–E3) (*𝄞 M1*)

Taking a closer look at all of the herbs and spices here is almost like making a journey around the world. Cooking courses are held in the rear section of the shop. A limited – but first-rate – selection of wines and spirits. *Mon–Fri 10am–8pm, Sat 10am–8pm | Prenzlauer Berg | Duncker-straße 9 | www.goldhahnundsampson.de | U 2 Eberswalderstraße*

INSIDER TIP ▶ KERNKRAFT BERLIN ☺ (146 C4) (*𝄞 P5*)

A paradise for squirrels and everybody else who loves nuts. The high shelves are loaded with stocks of wasabi and chilli peanuts, chocolate covered almonds and many other nibblpes from all over the world. If you like it a little less brittle, you can sink your teeth into the dried fruit or opt for the candied ginger – everything on offer can be sampled first! *Friedrichshain | Neue Bahnhofstraße 33 | www.kernkraft-berlin.de | S 5, 9, 75 Ostkreuz*

VEGANZ ☺ (138 C2) (*𝄞 O*)

Europe's first vegan supermarket offers a wide range of organic, ecologically pro-duced groceries and accessories. On Sun-days brunch *(11am–5pm)* in the café – try the richness of vegan meals (12.90 eu-ros/pers.). *Mon–Sat 9am–9pm | Prenz-lauer Berg | Schivelbeiner Str. 34 | tel. 030*

⭐ **Flea market am 17. Juni**
The classic among Berlin's flea markets → p. 81

⭐ **KaDeWe**
Even just visiting the gourmet floor is a great experience → p. 82

⭐ **Quartier 206**
Sophisticated atmosphere, fine selection – welcome to this designer departement store → p. 83

⭐ **14 oz.**
Not only VIPs like shopping here as if they were in a private living room → p. 83

⭐ **Trippen**
Wood and leather designer shoes of cult status; the cool showroom looks like a gallery → p. 84

⭐ **Sterling Gold**
Magnificent ball gowns with rhinestones and sequins from fifty years of design – this shop is a true treasure trove for retro fans → p. 85

⭐ **Markt am Maybachufer**
Large Turkish families buy vegetables by the crate, the merchants try to outshout each other → p. 85

MARCO POLO HIGHLIGHTS

44 03 60 48 | www.veganz.de | U-/S-Bahn Schönhauser Allee

WHISKY & CIGARS (133 E1) *(Ⓜ L3)*

A cosy shop with comfortable club armchairs where you can try out cigars from Cuba, the Dominican Republic and Honduras and take a sip or two of one of the 1000 varieties of whiskies on offer – Scottish malts, noble bourbons, blends – and rums. Tip: evening tasting sessions. *Mitte | Sophienstraße 8–9 | www.whisky-cigars.de | U 8 Weinmeierstraße*

THIS & THAT

INSIDER TIP ▶ AUS BERLIN
(133 F2) *(Ⓜ L3)*

Products from more than 200 Berlin designers add colour to the drab prefabricated concrete building opposite the Kaufhof department store. These range from painted storm jackets to heartbreak pills. You can even find Gorbachev Vodka on the shelves – this is produced in Reinickendorf. Sometimes, DJs work the turntables. *Mon–Sat 12noon–7pm | Mitte | Karl-Liebknecht-Straße 17 | www.ausberlin.de | U/S Alexanderplatz*

ECO SHOWROOM ☺
(133 F1) *(Ⓜ L3)*

Here you will find fair-trade products that have been produced ecologically: the cheerful shop has just about everything the environmentally-conscious buyer could desire from chic jackets made of hemp to furniture. *Mon–Sat from 12noon onwards | Mitte | Almstadtstr. 35 | www.eco-showroom.de | U 8 Weinmeisterstraße*

INTERSHOP 2000 (146 B4) *(Ⓜ O5)*

You will find (almost) everything that was part of everyday life in former East Germany in this erstwhile Konsum shop: Mitropa chinaware, eggcups and Free German Youth (FDJ) pennants. Ideal for rummaging around in the past era of Socialist design. *Wed–Fri 2–6pm, Sat, Sun 12noon–6pm | Friedrichshain | Danneckerstraße 8 | U/S Warschauer Straße*

KPM (131 D–E 1–2) *(Ⓜ F4)*

Elegant items from the Royal Porcelain Factory (KPM) are not only sold in the magnificently restored old buildings but also displayed in a fascinating way in special studios, with guided tours and special exhibitions. In an additional room on the other side of the courtyard you can purchase the somewhat cheaper B-goods. *Mon–Sat 10am–6pm | entrance fee KPM Welt 10 euros | Tiergarten | Wegelystr. 1 | www.kpm-berlin.de | S 7, 9, 75 Tiergarten*

LUXUS INTERNATIONAL
(138 C4) *(Ⓜ L2)*

120 Berlin designers display their latest products and wild ideas in this small shop. And there's no limit to these – you will find everything you can't do without, from cuddly-kebabs and badges for football-haters. The latest hit is a currywurst-stand card game. *Mon–Sat 11am until 8pm | Sun 1.30until 7.30pm | Prenzlauer Berg | Kastanienallee 101 | www.luxus international.de | U 2 Eberswaldestraße*

FLEA MARKETS

AM MAUERPARK
(138 C3) *(Ⓜ L1–2)*

Berlin's largest flea market not only offers any amount of second-hard goods and more-or-less valuable antiques and retro furniture, some young designers also sell their first collections here – usually printed T-shirts, jewellery and fashionable handbags. The public is hip and also spends a lot of time in the various beach bars on the site. *Sun 10am–5pm | Prenzlauer Berg | Eberswalder Straße | U 2 Eberswalder Straße*

BOXHAGENER PLATZ (146 C3) *(Ø O5)*
A small square in the eastern part of Friedrichshain with a quiet flea market, relatively low prices and a public of

FLEA MARKET AM 17. JUNI ★
(131 D–E2) *(Ø F–G4)*
The most famous flea market in the west of the city. The many professional antique,

Berlin's flea markets offer all kinds of useful and unusual second-hand articles

young people and students from the neighbourhood. The nearby cafés are ideal places to sit and watch the dealers and bargain-hunters. *Sun 10am–4pm | Friedrichshain | Boxhagener Platz | U5 Samariterstraße*

NOWKÖLLN FLEA MARKET
(153 E2–3) *(Ø M6)*
The 'in' flea market on Maybachufer with chic T-shirts by Berlin designers, retro second-hand stuff and other knick-knacks the hip people who live here need in their lofts. Live music and grilled sausages. *1st Sun in the month 9am–4pm | Neukölln | Maybachufer | www.nowkoelln.de | U8 Schönleinstraße*

clothing, jewellery, and record and CD dealers sometimes demand excessive prices. But here bartering is the order of the day. The second-hand dealers are in the upper section towards the Siegessäule and the arts and crafts people in the other direction near Ernst-Reuter-Platz. *Sat/Sun 10am–5pm | Charlottenburg | Straße des 17. Juni | S Tiergarten*

DEPARTMENT STORES

DUSSMANN (132 C3) *(Ø K4)*
This so-called 'cultural department store' boasts four floors of CDs, DVDs, videos, books, games and software. The many special offers will whet your appetite. You

FASHION

can listen to all of the CDs and other sound media in the music department. *Mon–Fri 10am until midnight, Sat 10am–11.30pm | Mitte | Friedrichstraße 90 | www.kulturkaufhaus.de | U/S Friedrichstraße*

GALERIES LAFAYETTE
(132 C4) (*Ⓜ K4*)
An eldorado for shoppers with a wonderful delicatessen department, international fashion and sensational architecture. *Mitte | Französische Str. 23 | U 6 Französische Straße*

FASHION

CACHE CŒUR (139 D5) (*Ⓜ L2*)
This is where vintage fashion by renowned Berlin designers is sold directly to men and women of the world. This is also where you can find unused fashion from times gone by including the 1960s; but this all has its price. Givenchy shoes, a dress by Alexander McQueen or fur caps and designer telephones – here, trends become history. *Tue–Fri 2pm–8pm, Sat 12noon–6pm | Prenzlauer Berg |*

Even those who don't buy anything cannot help but admire the domed round building of the Galeries Lafayette

KADEWE ★ ●
(131 F5) (*Ⓜ G5*)
It is worth visiting the KaDeWe just to go to the delicatessen department: the 7000m2 (1.7 acres) has (almost) everything from artichokes to zabaglione. The selection of high-fashion labels on the clothing floors is also overwhelming. *Schöneberg | Tauentzienstr. 21–24 | U 1, 2, 3 Wittenbergplatz*

Schönhauser Allee 174 | www.cachecoeur. de | U2 Senefelderplatz

DE LA REH ☺ (131 E5) (*Ⓜ G6*)
Green fashion – clothes and accessories made of ecologically-produced materials – plays first fiddle here. The styles and designs range from elegant to casual and you won't notice their alternative origins in any way at all. They are quite simply

'stylish'.Mon-Sat 11am-8pm / *Schöneberg | Nürnberger Str. 23 | www.delareh.de | U 1, 2, 3, Wittenbergplatz*

INSIDER TIP **NIX** (133 D2) *(ØØ K3)*
Discrete colours, robust materials and simple cuts are the secrets of Barbara Gebhardt's success. A Nix coat or skirt is just as suited for everyday wear as it is for visiting the opera. *Mitte | Oranienburger Str. 32 | www.nix.de | S 1, 2, 25 Oranienburger Straße*

QUARTIER 206 ★ (132 C5) *(ØØ K4)*
Elegant, designer shop with fashion by Cerruti, Yves Saint-Laurent, rive gauche, Strenesse, Gabriele Strehle, Gucci and others. There are bargains in the 'Department-Store'. *Mitte | Friedrichstraße 71 | U 6 Französische Straße*

TAUSENDSCHÖN ☺
(139 D3) *(ØØ M1)*
Lovingly decorated shop with colourful, trendy fashions. The jeans, sweatshirt jackets and skirts are not only made of organically grown cotton but are also dyed with natural colours and without using toxic chemicals. There are also ballerina shoes made out of hemp and natural-rubber wellies. *Mon–Sat 12noon–8pm | Prenzlauer Berg | Raumerstr. 12 | tram M2 Marienburger Straße*

THATCHERS (138 C4) *(ØØ L2)*
Black-and-white transparent fabrics and grey tones are the ingredients of these classical fashions that offer unexpected revelations. The absolute highlights are the evening and cocktail dresses: seductive, original! There is another branch in the Hackesche Höfe in Berlin Mitte. *Mon–Sat 11am–7pm | Prenzlauer Berg | Kastanienallee 21 | www.thatchers.de | U2 Eberswalder Straße*

THE CORNER
(133 D4) *(ØØ K4)*
Haute couture meets street wear and luxurious accessories. The huge shop on Gendarmenmarkt with a coffee bar will tempt you to stroll through its departments and gaze in awe at the jackets and dresses by Balenciaga, Chloé, YSL and Givenchy. There is a branch in Charlottenburg (Knesebeckstr. 32). *Mitte | Französische Straße 40/corner of Markgrafenstraße | www.thecornerberlin.de | U 6 Französische Straße*

WERTVOLL ☺ (139 E5) *(ØØ M2)*
Organic cotton, recycled materials and pine fibres are the basic ingredients for fashionable underwear, blouses and dresses. Labels such as People Tree, G=9,8 and Boa Studio guarantee fair production conditions and part of the profits from sales are donated to charitable organisations. *Prenzlauer Berg | Marienburger Straße 37 | www.wertvoll-berlin.com | tram M2 Marienburger Straße*

14 OZ. ★ (133 E2) *(ØØ L3)*
Mixture of fashionable brands and many bargains (jeans!). The shop is run by Karl-Heinz Müller, the initiator of the ,,Bread & Butter" fashion fair. If you prefer, you can make your purchases in the private atmosphere of a living room. Müller has had some rooms on the first floor set up especially for this purpose. *Mitte | Neue Schönhauser Str. 13 | www.14oz-berlin.com | U 8 Weinmeierstraße*

SHOES

INSIDER TIP **JÜNEMANNS PANTOFFEL-ECK** (139 D6) *(ØØ L3)*
Real felt slippers just like grandma used to wear are stacked to the ceiling of this small workroom-cum-shop. The products of the 100-year-old family business have

SECOND HAND

Trippen displays its shoes as if they were works of art

long developed a cult status of their own and are shipped abroad. *Mitte | Torstr. 39 | www.pantoffeleck.de | U2 Rosa-Luxemburg-Platz*

LUCCICO (138 C6) (*L3*)
Unusual design, fine workmanship and good value for money – all this leads to the house in the 'shopping Bermuda triangle' being full all the time. The two other branches are located at Oranienburger Str. 23 (outlet) and Bergmannstr. 8. *Mon–Fri 12noon–8pm, Sat 11am–4pm | Mitte | Weinmeisterstraße 12 | www.luccico.de | U 8 Weinmeisterstraße*

TRIPPEN ★ ☺
(133 E2) (*L3*)
Absolutely first-rate, designer wood and leather shoes that have created a furore throughout the world. The showroom with the models displayed under spotlights in individual niches is more reminiscent of a gallery than a shop. The company's motto is 'ecologically honest and anatomically sensible'. *Mitte | Rosenthaler Str. 40/41 | Hackesche Höfe IV & VI | www.trippen. com | S Hackescher Markt*

ZEHA (138 B5) (*K3*)
Berlin label with cult status with classic shoes made of calf leather and sneakers and court shoes of the highest quality. There are branches at Kurfürstendamm 188–89 (entrance Schlüterstraße) and Prenzlauer Allee 22. *Mon–Fri 12noon–8pm, Sat 10am–6pm | Mitte | Brunnenstr. 195 | www.zeha-berlin.de | U8 Rosenthaler Platz*

SECOND HAND

MADONNA
(130 A5) (*E5*)
A wide selection of exquisite designer and brand names. All of the Versace coats, Jil Sander pullovers and Chanel costumes seem to be new but are actually second hand. Bad buys on the part of their first owners? There is a branch with designer fashion for men at Mommsenstr. 43. *Mon–Fri 12noon–7pm Sat 11am–4pm | Charlottenburg | Mommsenstraße 57 | S Charlottenburg*

MEMORY (139 D5) (*L2*)
At first glance, this seems to be a chaotic mess of used suitcases, clothes and shoes.

If you look closer, the goods reveal themselves as high-quality originals from times gone by: Prada costumes from the 1980s or elegant 1970s checked dresses. With a café. *Mon–Sat 2–7pm | Prenzlauer Berg | Schwedter Str. 32 | U2 Senefelder Platz*

STERLING GOLD ★
(133 D2) (*ØJ K3*)

You will be dazzled by these glittering ball and evening gowns covered with rhinestones and sequins. There are also cashmere coats and all items can be altered to fit. *Mon–Fri 12noon–8pm, Sat 12noon–6pm | Mitte | Oranienburger Str. 32 Heckmann-Höfe | www.sterlinggold.de | S 1, 2, 25 Oranienburger Straße*

WEEKLY MARKETS

INSIDER TIP KARL-AUGUST-PLATZ ☺
(141 E5) (*ØJ E5*)

Specialities from all over Europe make this market a real delicatessen paradise. Cheese from the Alps and organic carrots, fresh noodles, jam and much more not only attract gourmets from Charlottenburg. *Wed 8am until 1pm, Sat 8am until 2pm | Charlottenburg | Karl-August-Platz | U 7 Wilmersdorfer Straße*

KOLLWITZMARKT ☺ (139 D4) (*ØJ M2*)

Many the local residents buy here; young families stock up on organic vegetables and meat and delicatessen delights from regional producers. Thu: organic food only; Sat: a wider selection. *Thu 12noon–7pm, Sat 9am–4pm | Prenzlauer Berg | Kollwitzplatz | U2 Senefelder Platz*

MARKT AM MAYBACHUFER ★ ● ☺
(147 E2–3) (*ØJ M6*)

Everything the large Anatolian family needs can be bought at the 'Turkish market'. Grapes, tomatoes and aubergines

are sold by the crate. The young German smart set from Kreuzberg are more attracted to antipasti and organic cheese. *Tue, Fri 12noon until 6.30pm | Neukölln | Maybachufer | U 8 Schönleinstraße*

WINTERFELDTMARKT
(151 D2) (*ØJ H6*)

Visiting this weekly market is an absolute must in the Schöneberg gay and academic scene. And afterwards just watch the world go by from one of the cafés. *Wed 8am–2pm, Sat 8am–4pm | Schöneberg | Winterfeldtplatz | 1, 2 Nollendorfplatz*

LOW BUDGET

▶ For retro fans: *Arm & Sexy* **(153 E4)** (*ØJ M7*) (Wed 2pm–7pm, Thu 2pm–6pm, Fri 2pm–7pm, Sat 12noon–5pm | Reuterstraße 62 | www.arm-und-sexy.de | U 7 Hermannplatz) in Neukölln has everything from radios to eggcups from the 1930s to 1970s.

▶ The *Marc-O'Polo-Outlet* **(140 C4)** (*ØJ D4*) (Mon–Fri 10am–6.30pm | Kaiserdamm 7 | U 2 Sophie-Charlotte-Platz) is a haven for bargain hunters.

▶ *Maaßen 10* **(151 D2)** (*ØJ L1*) (Mon–Fri 10am–7pm, Sat 10am–6pm | Maaßenstraße 10 | U 1, 2 Nollendorfplatz) has inexpensive jeans and shirts from last season.

▶ *Logo An- und Verkauf* **(146 A3)** (*ØJ K7*) (Mon–Fri 12noon–7pm, Sat 10am–4pm | Bergmannstraße 10 | U7 Gneisenaustraße) offers reasonably priced new and used CDs and records; indie, pop, rock, hip-hop.

ENTERTAINMENT

CITY — WHERE TO START?

If you want to have a good time and not spend much money, the Neukölln district around **Weserstraße** is the place to go *(U7, 8 Hermannstraße)*. You will find many popular bars and clubs (including *Riva Bar* and *Weekend Club*) in Mitte between **Alexanderplatz** and **Hackescher Markt** or around the **Oberbaumbrücke**. At *Watergate*, you can dance with a view of the Spree. Nearby, the queues in front of *Berghain* show you that this is one of the best clubs in the world.

In Berlin, nights are not only for sleeping: dance to the early hours, sit as long as you like with your beer at the bar, visit concerts or theatre performances, go to the cinema – that gets locals and tourists in the right mood and ready to party the night away.

Hardly anywhere else in the world is there a larger number of clubs, bars and cultural venues than in Berlin. Almost 200 clubs, 30 cabarets and variety theatres, more than 130 cinemas and countless pubs and bars all compete with each other.

The council offices in Mitte district are not very generous about granting licences in some streets so that the locals can have

First stop, a theatre performance and then on to a bar and later dancing until dawn

some peace at night. And every year there are disputes between people living above a pub and its guests about the excessive noise that comes from nocturnal chatter outside in the open. So far, however, pub-owners have usually managed to defend their interests. Even those who want to sleep will wake up sooner or later – and then (for some) it's off for a quick beer round the corner to work up an appetite for the night to come!

BARS

BILLY WILDER'S
(143 F4) (*∅ J5*)
The selection of 85 different vodkas is unique and, supposedly, unequalled in Berlin. But, the (120 different!) cocktails are also exceptional. Chic surroundings with art-deco elements. Ideal after you have visited one of the nearby cinemas or musical theatres.

BARS

Closed Sun | Tiergarten | Potsdamer Straße 2 | tel. 030 26 55 48 60 | www. billywilders.de | U/S Potsdamer Platz

CSA (146 A2) *(𝄞 N4)*

Top address for design fans where Russian architecture meets modern minimalism. With a perfectly mixed Mai Tai in your

KUSCHLOWSKI (153 E–F4) *(𝄞 M7)*

Small living-room bar with a fireplace. One of the owners is a Russian woman who ensures that the vodka flows, served in a variety of different ways. *Daily from 8pm | Neukölln | Weserstraße 202 | tel. 0176 24 38 97 01 | www.kuschlowski.de | U 7, 8 Hermannplatz*

Stylish bar where you can still feel at home: Riva on Dircksenstraße

hand, you can watch what is happening on the magnificent boulevard or sink into one of the deep leather chairs in the lounge area. *Mon–Sat from 8pm | Friedrichshain | Karl-Marx-Allee 96 | tel. 030 29 04 47 41 | www.csa-bar.de | U 5 Weberwiese*

GAINSBOURG ★ (130 C4) *(𝄞 F5)*

This American-style bar is a location from home for Charlottenburg's bohemians where they sip first-rate cocktails and listen to music by the French namegiver. *Daily from 4pm | Charlottenburg | Jeanne-Mammen-Bogen 567–577 | tel. 030 3 13 74 64 | S Savignyplatz | www. gainsbourg.de*

NEWTON
(132 C5) *(𝄞 K4)*

The nude photographs by Helmut Newton might distract you from your oysters, champagne and cocktails. There is a cigar lounge on the first floor for those so inclined. *Sun–Thu 10am–3am, Fri, Sat 10am–4am | Mitte | Charlottenstraße 57 | tel. 030 20 29 54 21 | www.newton-bar.de | U 6 Französische Straße*

RIVA (133 E2) *(𝄞 L3)*

Guests sit at oval tables under a railway arch; the bottle rack in the centre is modelled on the *Titanic*. This is the place for aesthetes with a fondness for cultivated cocktails. *Daily from 6pm | Mitte | Dircksenstraße 142 | tel. 030 24 72 26 88 | www. riva-berlin.de | S-Bahn Hackescher Markt*

SOLAR ★ ☆ (152 A1) *(⑭ J5)*
It's great fun to drink your cocktails on the 16th floor and look down on the city. Especially, after the trip in a glass lift up the façade of the building has given you your first thrill! By the way, you can also enjoy a Mediterranean meal here. *Daily from 6pm | Kreuzberg | Stresemannstr. 76 | tel. 0163 7 65 27 00 | www.solar-berlin.de | S 1, 25 Anhalter Bahnhof*

STRANDBAR MITTE ● (133 D2) *(⑭ K3)*
This is where young and old meet on the banks of the Spree in summer to order their cocktails, coffee or beer from the self-service bar and relax in the deckchairs with a view towards the Museumsinsel. *May until Sept daily from 10am | Mitte | Monbijoustr. 3 | www.strandbar-mitte.de | S 1, 25 Oranienburger Straße*

INSIDER TIP WEINBAR RUTZ
(144 A1) *(⑭ K3)*
1001 wines lie waiting for you in the racks of this carefully-styled bar. The menu is as long as your arm but a sommelier will help you make your choice: in addition, exquisite cooking. *Tue–Sat 4pm–11pm | Mitte | Chausseestr. 8 | tel. 030 24 62 87 60 | www.rutz-weinbar.de | U6 Oranienburger Tor*

CLUBS

ADAGIO (132 A6) *(⑭ J5)*
Gigantic nightclub underneath the Theater am Potsdamer Platz. It is impossible to be bored in these cheerful Baroque-style surroundings which include five bars and a large dance floor. *Fri from 11pm, Sat from 10pm/entrance fee 10 euros | Tiergarten | Marlene-Dietrich-Platz 1 | tel. 030 258 98 90 | www.adagio. de | U/S Potsdamer Platz*

A TRANE (130 C4) *(⑭ F5)*
The unpretentiously-styled jazz club has live performances – every day! The concerts are always well-attended; reasonable entrance fees. *Daily from 9pm | Charlottenburg | Bleibtreustraße 1/corner of Pestalozzistraße | tel. 030 3 13 25 50 | www.a-trane. de | S Savignyplatz*

★ **Gainsbourg**
American bar in the heart of Charlottenburg with first-rate cocktails → p. 88

★ **Solar**
Club on the 16th floor with spectacular view over Berlin → p. 89

★ **Berghain/Panoramabar**
Internationally popular bar in a disused heating plant → p. 90

★ **Tausend**
Cool interior design; great drinks and DJs → p. 91

★ **Bar jeder Vernunft**
Top quality shows, variety performances and cooking in the mirror tent → p. 91

★ **Friedrichstadtpalast**
Glitz and glamour: the world's largest show stage with fabulous dancers → p. 94

★ **Philharmonie**
A must for classic fans: magnificent acoustics in 'Karajan's circus' → p. 95

★ **Deutsches Theater**
As in its best days: top-quality classics → p. 97

MARCO POLO HIGHLIGHTS

BERGHAIN/PANORAMABAR

⭐ (146 A3) (*ω N5*)

Techno-electro club that now has fans from all over the world. Night-owls between 20 and 40 have fun on the two floors of this disused heating plant with 18 m (60 ft) high ceilings and refuel at one of the four bars. All this with art on the walls and a laid-back atmosphere. *Fri, Sat from midnight | entrance fee 12 euros | Friedrichshain | Am Wriezener Bahnhof | S Ostbahnhof*

COOKIES (132 C4) (*ω K4*)

A Berlin institution: this is where the young crowd lets its hair down in a former cinema listening to Electro and House music and drinking cocktails. *Tue, Thu from 10pm | entrance fee 12 euros | Mitte | Unter den Linden/Friedrichstr. | U 6 Französische Straße*

INSIDER TIP ▶ **HAFENBAR** (138 A5) (*ω J3*)

Fun interior with ships' ropes, aquariums and portholes. Dance freaks between the ages of 20 and 50 cavort at ABBA parties, hit-parade and rock-'n-roll events. If you need to cool off, there are cocktails and schnapps instead of seawater. *Only on Fridays (German pop from 9pm) and Saturdays (mixed music from 10pm) | entrance fee 6–8 euros | Mitte | Chausseestr. 20 | tel. 030 2 82 85 93 | www.hafenbar-berlin.de | U 6 Naturkundemuseum*

PURO 🌿 (131 E–F4) (*ω G5*)

Sky-lounge on the 20th floor of the Europa Center with a dance floor and Japanese-inspired interior for those over 20. Great view over the city! *Thu, Fri from 9pm, Sat from 11pm | entrance fee 8 euros | Charlottenburg | Tauentzienstraße 11 | tel. 030 26 36 78 75 | www.puro-berlin.de | U1, 2, 3 Wittenbergplatz*

QUASIMODO (131 D4) (*ω F5*)

Traditional jazz club with concerts by well-known musicians. Almost all of the world-famous funk, soul and jazz stars – from Defunkt to Jasper van't Hof – have played here. *Daily from 9pm | entrance fee 12–22 euros | Charlottenburg | Kantstr. 12a | tel. 030 3 12 80 86 | www.quasimodo.de | U/S Zoologischer Garten*

SPINDLER & KLATT IN DER HEERESBÄCKEREI (146 A4) (*ω N5*)

Club restaurant with lounge atmosphere and a touch of Asia in an old warehouse. You eat lying down and this can sometimes mean that you will hear the crashed out night-owl on the sofa next to you snoring. Lovely terrace on the Spree. *Mid-May–Mid-Sept daily (in winter, Wed–Sun)*

LOW BUDGET

▶ The free concerts of the students from the *Hanns Eisler Music College* at *Charlottenstr. 55* **(144 A4)** (*ω K4*) (*U 2, 6 Stadtmitte*) and *Schlossplatz 7* **(133 E4)** (*ω L4*) (*U 2 Hausvogtei-platz*) locations present the virtuosos of the future / *tel. 030 2 03 09 21 01 | www.hfm-berlin.de*

▶ On Tuesdays, ticket prices are reduced to around 6 euros in the *Cinestar Centres* (for address see local press).

▶ The *Sageclub* **(145 D4)** (*ω M5*) (*Köpenicker Str. 76 | tel. 030 2 78 98 30 | www.sage-club.de | U 8 Heinrich-Heine-Straße*) presents 'Rock at Sage' (*Thu 7pm–10pm*) – free of charge.

▶ The *frannz-Club* **(139 D4)** (*ω L2*) (*Schönhauser Allee 36 | tel. 030 7 26 27 93 33 | www.frannz.de | U 2 Eberswalder Straße*) presents Indie-poprock for 4 euros on Thursdays.

food from 8pm, club Fri, Sat from 11pm | entrance fee 8 euros | Kreuzberg | Köpenicker Straße 16-17 | tel. 030 3 19 88 18 6 | www. spindlerklatt.com | U 1 Schlesisches Tor

TAUSEND ⭐ (132 B3) *(𝄞 J4)*

Perfectly mixed drinks and a discreet, elegant interior straight out of a James Bond film, along with a wall installation in the form of a gigantic eye. DJs from the dub and electro scene take care of the background sound. *Daily 9am–4.30pm and 6.30pm–midnight, breakfast 9am–10am | entrance fee 0–12 euros | Mitte | Schiffbauerdamm 11 | tel. 030 27 58 20 70 | www.tausendberlin.com | U/S Friedrichstraße*

TRESOR
(145 D4) *(𝄞 M5)*

International techno DJs sit at the turntables in this former heating plant. A 30 m (110 ft) long tunnel leads to the dance floor in the cellar. Rough industrial atmosphere and the noise level is nothing for sensitive souls. The young crowd is international. *Wed, Fri, Sat from 11pm | entrance fee 12 euros | Mitte | Köpenicker Str. 59–73 | tel. 030 8 90 64 20 | www. tresorberlin.de | U 8 Heinrich-Heine-Straße*

WATERGATE ≈
(146 A5) *(𝄞 N5–6)*

The last dancing stop before the Spree. A great view of the water and Oberbaumbrücke make this a popular place for well-heeled 25 to 40-year-olds to amuse themselves with drum-'n-bass and soul rhythms in carefully-styled modern surroundings. *Wed, Fri, Sat from midnight | entrance fee 6–12 euros | Kreuzberg | Falckensteinstraße 49 | tel. 030 61 28 03 94 | www. water-gate.de | U1 Schlesisches Tor*

WEEKEND (145 D2) *(𝄞 L–M3)*

Dancing on the 12th floor of the former 'Haus des Reisens' East German travel

In 'Bar jeder Vernunft'

organisation. Fans of house music between the ages of 20 and 40 amuse themselves high up above Alexanderplatz. The ≈ terrace and bar on the 15th floor are only open in summer – and then, the view is magnificent. *Thu, Fri, Sat from 11pm | entrance fee 10–15 euros | Mitte | Alexanderplatz 5 | www.week-end-berlin. de | U/S Alexanderplatz*

SHOWS & CABARET

BAR JEDER VERNUNFT ⭐
(131 E6) *(𝄞 F6)*

It is worth visiting this cabaret just to see the extravagant Jugendstil mirrortent. But, the innovative programme with stars from the chanson and comedy world such as Max Raabe and the Geschwister Pfister also have a lot going for them. You can eat and drink while you enjoy the performance. *Box office Mon–Sat 12noon–*

6.30pm, Sun 3pm–5.30pm | tickets 19–37 euros | Wilmersdorf | Schaperstr. 24 | tel. 030 8 83 15 82 | www.bar-jeder-vernunft.de | U 1, 9 Spichernstraße

DIE STACHELSCHWEINE
(131 E–F4) (*𝄞 G5*)

This political cabaret full of wit and verve is an institution in West Berlin. *Tickets 13–28 euros | Charlottenburg | Taunetzienstraße 9–12 | Europa Center | tel. 030 2 61 47 95 | www.stachelschweine-berlin.de | U 9, 15 Kurfürstendamm*

DISTEL (132 C3) (*𝄞 K3–4*)

This establishment has been in existence for more than 50 years and while the Wall was still standing its performers were complete masters at covertly criticising the East German system. Today, capitalism is the target of their irony – but it is still amusing. *Box office Mon–Fri 11am–6pm, Sat/Sun 11am–5pm | tickets 13–29 euros | Mitte | Friedrichstraße 10 | tel. 030 2 04 47 04 | U/S Friedrichstraße*

TIPI, DAS ZELT (143 E3) (*𝄞 H4*)

Well-known entertainment stars such as Georgette Dee and Tim Fischer appear here as do up-and-coming a-cappella-ensembles and virtuoso African drummers. Rustic atmosphere in a marquee next to the Federal Chancellery. *Tiergarten | Große Querallee | ticket tel. 030 39 06 65 50 | www.tipi-das-zelt.de | S 1, 2 Brandenburger Tor*

INSIDER TIP ▸ UFA-FABRIK
(157 D4) (*𝄞 J10*)

The whole universe of off-culture on the former premises of the Ufa film company: a circus for children to take part in, cabaret, variety shows. *Tempelhof | Viktoriastr. 13 | tel. 030 75 50 30 | www.ufafabrik.de | U6 Ullsteinstraße*

CINEMAS

The approximately 300 cinemas of all sizes and categories attract their audiences with their diversified programmes. You can find a list of what is showing in

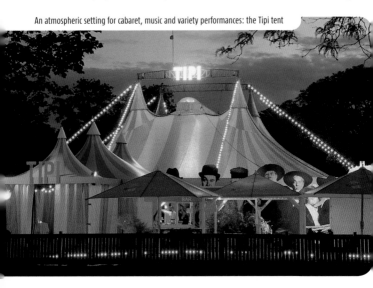

An atmospheric setting for cabaret, music and variety performances: the Tipi tent

each individual cinemas (along with their addresses) in the Berlin events magazines *Zitty* and *tip*.

PUBS

DIENER – TATTERSALL
(130 C4) (*ØJ F5*)
Many of the former and current guests, from Billy Wilder to Helmut Newton, have been immortalised in photographs. This is still a popular place for actors and bohemians to drop by for a glass of beer or for a plate of meatballs with mustard. But, of course less famous guests are also welcome. *Daily from 6pm | Charlottenburg | Grolmanstr. 47 | tel. 030 8 81 53 29 | www. diener-tattersall.de | S Savignyplatz*

INSIDERTIP ▶ KACHELLOUNGE
(153 F4) (*ØJ N7*)
One of the cosiest pubs in Berlin is decorated with old stoves tiles and furnished with sofas. Its mainly young guests reward this by coming regularly and it is usually crowded by midnight at the latest. *Daily from 7.30pm | Neukölln | Weichselstr. 54 | U7 Rathaus Neukölln*

LEMKE (133 E2) (*ØJ L3*)
The rustic brewery in railway arch number 143 offers a lot of different beers and hearty food from the grill. Beer garden in summer. *Daily from 12noon, Mon–Fri lunch buffet 12noon–3pm | Mitte | Dircksenstraße | tel. 030 24 72 87 27 | www. brauhaus-lemke.de | S Hackescher Markt*

MÖBEL OLFE (153 D2) (*ØJ M6*)
At night, things really start to happen at one of the ugliest places in town, the rundown Zentrum Kreuzberg at Kottbusser Tor. The later it gets, the more Polish beer and vodka flows down the guests' parched throats. Mixed hetero and gay clientele. *Tue–Sun from 6pm | Kreuzberg |* *Dresdener Str. 177 | tel. 030 23 27 46 90 | www.moebel-olfe.de | U1, 8 Kottbusser Tor*

RESTAURATION SOPHIEN 11
(133 E1) (*ØJ L3*)
Comfy pub with an inner courtyard next to the Hackesche Höfe where you can relax over reasonably-priced meatballs and beer. *Daily from 5pm | Mitte | Sophienstr. 11 | tel. 030 2 83 21 36 | www. sophien-elf.de | S Hackescher Markt*

ROCK-'N'-ROLL-HERBERGE
(153 F1) (*ØJ M5*)
Even if you do not stay in this home-away-from home for musicians, you will be welcome to drink a beer and play billiards or table football in the foyer. Maybe you'll meet one of tomorrow's rock stars. And, if you can't make it home, just book a room for the night. *Sun–Thu 9am–4am, Fri, Sat 9am–7am | Kreuzberg | Muskauer Str. 11 | tel. 030 61 62 36 00 | www.rock-n-roll-herberge.de | U1 Görlitzer Bahnhof*

STÄNDIGE VERTRETUNG
(132 B3) (*ØJ K3–4*)
When the government moved to Berlin, many people from the Rhineland came with it. This is where lively ex-Bonners get together for a glass of Kölsch beer and celebrate carnival the way they did it back home. *Daily from 9am | Mitte | Schiffbauerdamm 8 | tel. 030 2 82 39 65 | U/S Friedrichstraße*

YORCKSCHLÖSSCHEN ● (152 A3) (*ØJ J6*)
'A bit run-down but still cosy' is the how regulars swigging their beer or listing to a live concert feel about this place. Lovely beer garden in summer. One of the oldest and most-popular jazz pubs in the city. *Mon–Sat 5pm–3am, Sun from 10am | Kreuzberg | Yorckstraße 15 | tel. 030 20 15 80 70 | www.yorckschloesschen.de | U 6, 7 Mehringdamm*

CONCERTS, MUSICALS, DANCE & OPERA

CONCERTS, MUSICALS, DANCE & OPERA

ADMIRALPALAST (132 C3) (*ID K3–4*)
New life has been breathed into the former entertainment palace from 1911: plays, musicals and theatre sport brighten up the stage near Friedrichstraße Station. *Mitte | Friedrichstraße 101 | tel. 030 47 99 74 99 | U/S Friedrichstraße*

DEUTSCHE OPER (130 A2) (*ID E4*)
Once the West's answer to the State Opera in the East. Today, a house with a unconventional interpretations. *Charlottenburg | Bismarckstraße 35 | tel. 030 34 38 43 43 | www.deutscheoperberlin.de | U2 Deutsche Oper*

FRIEDRICHSTADTPALAST ★
(132 C2) (*ID K3*)
Germany's only – and the world's largest – revue theatre with plenty of glamour and high-kicking dancing girls. *Mitte | Friedrichstraße 107 | tel. 030 23 26 23 26 | www.friedrichstadtpalast.de | U6 Oranienburger Tor*

GRIPS THEATER (131 F1) (*ID G4*)
A Berlin institution that shows socio-critical musicals for the city's youth and adults who have remained young. Volker Ludwig's musical set in the underground 'Linie 1' has been playing for 25 years and its successor 'Linie 2 – der Alptraum' has guaranteed 24 hours a day a full house since 2009. *Moabit | Altonaer Str. 22 / in the Hansaplatz underground station | tel. 030 3 97 47 40 | www.grips-theater.de | U9 Hansaplatz*

HEBBEL AM UFER (152 A2) (*ID K6*)
Experimental concept focussing mainly on dance. Various avantgarde productions and guest performances in three theatres. *HAU 1 (Stresemannstr. 29), HAU 2 (Hallesches Ufer 32), HAU 3 (Tempelhofer Ufer 10) | tel. 030 25 90*

BOOKS & FILMS

▶ **Berlin Blues** – The author and musician Sven Regener (founder of the Element of Crime band) captured the zeitgeist in West Berlin just before the Wall fell in this novel

▶ **Russian Disco** – Wladimir Kaminer, from whom the 'Russian Disco' in Kaffee Burger originates, demonstrates his keen observation of everyday life in East Berlin in the 1990s in this and other books

▶ **Berlin Alexanderplatz** – This classic novel by Alfred Döblin was first published in 1929 and is still highly recommended reading. The story of an ordinary person attempting to get back on the tracks after being released from prison is just as pertinent today – Rainer Werner Fassbinder's film with Günter Lamprecht in the main role has become a legend

▶ **Run Lola Run** – Tom Tykwer's 1998 success shows Berliners as the really are: always in a hurry and always out of money

▶ **Good Bye Lenin!** – Wolfgang Becker's prize-winning film (2003) about life in an East Berlin flat at the time of reunification – told with humour and a sense of tragedy

Festive surroundings for superb opera performances: Staatsoper Unter den Linden

04 27 | www.hebbel-am-ufer.de | U 1, 6 Hallesches Tor

KONZERTHAUS AM GENDARMENMARKT (133 D5) (𝔐 K4)

Today, the Konzerthaus Orchestra, the former Berlin Symphony Orchestra, is the main performer in what was originally a theatre built by Schinkel between 1818 and 1821. One drawback, however, the acoustics are not ideal everywhere. *Advance sales Mon–Sat 12noon–7pm, Sun 12noon until 4pm | Mitte | Am Gendarmenmarkt | tel. 030 2 03 09 21 01 | www.konzerthaus-berlin.de | U 2, 6 Stadtmitte*

INSIDERTIP NEUKÖLLNER OPER (153 F6) (𝔐 N8)

A comparatively small theatre with amusing performances and unconventional interpretations of light operas and musical plays. A real off-opera! *Neukölln | Karl-Marx-Str. 131 | tel. 030 68 89 07 77 | www.neukoellneroper.de | U 7 Karl-Marx-Straße*

PHILHARMONIE ⭐ (143 E4) (𝔐 J5)

This is the home of the Berlin Philharmonic Orchestra and its principal conductor Sir Simon Rattle. The acoustics in the building designed by the architect Hans Scharoun are first-rate. ● INSIDERTIP Free concerts at 1 pm on Tuesdays from September to June! *Advance sales Mon–Fri 3 until 6pm, Sat, Sun 11am until 2pm | Tiergarten | Matthäikirchstraße 1 | tel. 030 25 48 89 99 | www.philharmonie.de | U/S Potsdamer Platz*

STAATSOPER UNTER DEN LINDEN (133 D4) (𝔐 K4)

The once magnificent interior of Berlin's oldest opera house has seen better days and it will be renovated by 2015. Until then, performances – many of them conducted by the house's principal conductor Daniel Barenboim – will be given in the *Schillertheater (Charlottenburg | Bismarckstraße 110). Mitte | Unter den Linden 7 | tel. 030 20 35 45 55 | www.staatsoper-berlin. de | U 6 Französische Straße*

THEATER DES WESTENS
(131 D4) (*ΩΩ F5*)
Musical theatre. The house opened in the 19th century and many stars, including Josephine Baker and Hildegard Knef, have performed here. *Charlottenburg | Kantstraße 12 | ticket hotline tel. 01805 44 44 (*) | www.stage-entertainment.de | U/S Zoologischer Garten*

THEATER AM POTSDAMER PLATZ
(132 A6) (*ΩΩ J5*)
Popular musical theatre. Currently, 'Hinterm Horizont' (Beyond the Horizon) with hits by Udo Lindenberg is being performed. The play about an East-West love affair was developed by old-rocker Udo himself. *Tiergarten | Marlene-Dietrich-Platz 1 | tel. 01805 44 44 (*) | www.stage-entertainment.de | U/S Potsdamer Platz*

DANCE

GRÜNER SALON
(133 F1) (*ΩΩ L3*)
Thursday night is tango time in a side wing of the Volksbühne theatre when an orchestra starts swinging. *Tue: salsa; Sat: concerts. Mitte | Rosa-Luxemburg-Platz | tel. 030 6 88 33 23 90 | www.gruenersalon.de | U 2 Rosa-Luxemburg-Platz*

HAVANA (151 D4) (*ΩΩ H7*)
There are separate areas for salsa, meringue, bachata and black music; so you can change your rhythm whenever you feel like it and the chilled drinks keep you in a good mood. Wed (only salsa,

SPORTING FEVER

Football fans head for the *Olympia Stadium* that was completely renovated for the 2006 World Championship (p. 55). This is where the professionals from Hertha BSC play. There are fan shops in all of the major department stores in Berlin. Tickets online or from *tel. 030 3 00 92 80 (*)*. The main office is in the *Olympia Stadium* **(156 C3)** (*ΩΩ A4*) *(Hanns-Braun-Straße | Friesenhaus II | tel. 030 3 00 92 80 | www.herthabsc.de)*. The second-league team FC Union *(www.fc-union-berlin.de)* plays in the *An der Alten Försterei* stadium **(157 E4)** (*ΩΩ O*) out in Köpenick. Tickets can be purchased at most booking offices as well as online.

The national-league basketball team *Alba Berlin (www.albaberlin.de)* is a must if you are interested in the sport. Home games are played in the *O₂ World Arena* **(146 A4)** (*ΩΩ N5*) *(Mühlenstr. 12–30)* in Friedrichshain. Tickets under *tel. 01805 57 00 11 (*)* and in the Max-Schmeling-Halle **(138 C3)** (*ΩΩ L1*) *(Mon–Fri 10am–7pm, Sat 12noon–5pm | Am Falkplatz | ticket tel. 030 44 30 44 30.* Ice hockey fans won't want to miss a game by the speedy *Polar Bears Berlin (www.eisbaeren.de)*. Tickets for DEL games: *tel: 030 97 18 40 40* or online. Their home stadium is also the *O₂ World* at Ostbahnhof (see above).

from 9pm) and Fri, Sat (from 10pm) *Schöneberg | Hauptstraße 30 | tel. 030 784 85 65 | www.havanna-berlin.de | U 7 Kleistpark*

THEATRE

Berlin has a great reputation as an important theatre city. Stage personalities who make it here have reached the pinnacle of the German theatre world.

BERLINER ENSEMBLE
(132 B–C2) *(Ø J–K3)*
This is where Bertolt Brecht used to work. His plays are still a staple of its repertoire but other playwrights are also performed. Popular; often sold out. *Mitte | Bertolt-Brecht-Platz 1 | tel. 030 28 40 81 55 | www. berliner-ensemble.de | U/S Friedrichstraße*

DEUTSCHES THEATER ★
(132 B2) *(Ø J3)*
This was Germany's most famous theatre 100 years ago when Max Reinhardt was its director. Today, attempts are being made to pick up the threads of a glorious past. Many classical plays in the repertoire. *Mitte | Schumannstr. 13a | tel. 030 28 44 12 25 | www.deutschestheater.de | U 6 Oranienburger Tor*

MAXIM GORKI THEATER
(133 D3) *(Ø K4)*
Ambitious plays by young authors as well as classics. The highly-committed ensemble does not limit itself to Russian dramas. *Mitte | Am Festungsgraben 2 | tel. 030 20 22 11 15 | www.gorki.de | S Hackescher Markt*

SCHAUBÜHNE
(149 D2) *(Ø E6)*
Today, the ensemble of the legendary Schaubühne, which achieved cult status when Peter Stein was its director, com-

Creative and inspirational: performances in the 'Sophiensaele'

petes with the Volksbühne with its performances of socio-critical, unconventional plays. *Wilmersdorf | Kurfürstendamm 153 | tel. 030 89 00 23 | www.schaubuehne.de | U 7 Adenauerplatz*

INSIDER TIP ▶ SOPHIENSAELE
(133 E1) *(Ø L3)*
The equipment is rather basic but the creative spirit is all the more productive. It is amazing to see how it is possible to produce dramas that really get under your skin with such limited resources. *Mitte | Sophienstr. 18 | tel. 030 2 83 52 66 | www. sophiensaele.com | S Hackescher Markt*

VOLKSBÜHNE (133 F1) *(Ø L3)*
Stage director Frank Castorf is something of a cult figure in Germany and he, and others, try to be provocative with their unconventional productions. *Mitte | Rosa-Luxemburg-Platz | tel. 030 24 06 57 77 | www.volksbuehne-berlin.de | U 2 Rosa-Luxemburg-Platz*

WHERE TO STAY

If there is one branch in Berlin that is really booming, it is tourism. Even while the Wall was still standing there were hardly ever as many guests in the city as there have been in recent years. Hotels are springing up everywhere.

Berlin has approximately 117,000 beds waiting for its guests! And, some of the architecture is also quite impressive. Designer hotels such as the Q! or the Grand Hyatt with its spa high above the roofs of the city on Potsdamer Platz set new standards in architecture and interior design. The Radisson Blu opposite Berliner Dom is another highlight. The lobby is crowned by a six-storey aquarium one can pass through in the lift. The many small guest-houses in the city don't need these kinds of frills; they have an advantage that cannot be bought – personal atmosphere! Many guests appreciate seeing the host or hostess standing at the stove in the morning preparing breakfast more than the most luxurious buffet.

The enormous choice of hostels, private rooms and flats means that is cheaper to stay in Berlin than in most other cities. Some have branches located throughout the city but the small, privately-run hotels and guesthouses are also popular. Even if you have limited resources, you will be able to spend the night in comfort.

Hotel information: *tel. 030 25 00 25 | http:// www.visitberlin.de.* A list of hotels can be

Photo: Hotel de Rome on Bebelplatz

Berlin's hotels try to outdo each other when it comes to luxury and service, but the smaller, less lavish establishments are also prospering

obtained by telephoning Berlin Tourism Marketing at the same number or, in writing, from: *Berlin Tourismus & Kongress GmbH | Am Karlsbad 11 | 10785 Berlin*

HOTELS: EXPENSIVE

BRISTOL HOTEL KEMPINSKI BERLIN
(131 D5) *(∅ F5)*
The classic on Kurfürstendamm. After a stroll through the city, its guests can relax

in great comfort. It also has Berlin's largest Presidential Suite on two floors. *301 rooms and suites | Charlottenburg | Kurfürstendamm 27 | tel. 030 88 43 40 | www.kem pinski-berlin.de | U 1 Uhlandstraße*

ELLINGTON ★ (131 E5) *(∅ G5)*
Informally elegant, comfortable hotel that welcomes families with its idyllic summer garden in the inner courtyard. One child under the age of twelve may stay

in the room of two full-paying adults free of charge; there is a charge of 25 euros for each additional child. *285 rooms and suites | Schöneberg | Nürnberger Straße 50–55 | tel. 030 68 31 50 | www.ellington-hotel.de | U1, 2, 3 Wittenbergplatz*

Ready for an elevator ride in an aquarium? Go to the Radisson Blue

NHOW ⭐ (146 B4) (*M N–O5*)
Many creative guests are attracted by Karim Rashid's cool design and the fact that sound studios can be rented. The retro-

futuristic interior of the hotel's Fabrics Restaurant on the banks of the Spree reminds one of a mixture between Alice in Wonderland and Star Trek. *304 rooms | Friedrichshain | Stralauer Allee 3 | tel. 030 2 90 29 90 | www.nh-hotels.de | U/S Warschauer Straße*

Q! ⭐ (130 C5) (*M L3*)
Sweeping lounge design – even the reception looks like a cocktail bar. Award-winning and widely acclaimed. *72 rooms, 4 studios, 1 penthouse | Charlottenburg | Knesebeckstraße 67 | tel. 030 8 10 06 60 | www.loock-hotels.com/qhotel | U1 Uhlandstraße*

RADISSON BLU ⭐
(133 E3) (*M L4*)
The five-star hotel is located on the banks of the Spree directly opposite Berliner Dom. The largest cylindrical aquarium in the world with a million litres of water is located in the lobby. A lift from the Sea-Life Aquarium passes through the underwater world up to the sixth floor. *427 rooms | Mitte | Karl-Liebknecht-Str. 3 | tel. 030 23 82 80 | www.berlinradissonblu.com | S Hackescher Markt*

HOTELS: MODERATE

ARTE LUISE KUNSTHOTEL
(132 A–B 2–3) (*M J3*)
Creative atmosphere: each room has been individually decorated by a different artist. But comfort and homeliness also get their due. Not only artists stay here – it is also popular with 'normal' visitors to Berlin. *50 rooms | Mitte | Luisenstraße 19 | tel. 030 28 44 80 | www.luise-berlin.com | U/S Friedrichstraße*

ARTEMISIA
(149 E2) (*M E6*)
This hotel on the top floors of an old, modernised building is exclusively for women.

Tastefully decorated rooms and a roof-top terrace for relaxing after your discovery tour of Berlin. *19 rooms | Wilmersdorf | Brandenburgische Straße 18 | tel. 030 873 89 05 | www.frauenhotel.info | U 7 Konstanzer Straße*

BOGOTA
(130 B5) (*ØJ E6*)

Peaceful hotel near Kurfürstendamm. Many regular guests, respectable rooms, personal atmosphere, friendly service. *116 rooms | Charlottenburg | Schlüterstr. 45 | tel. 030 8 81 50 01 | www.hotel-bogata.de | U 7 Adenauerplatz*

DORINT NOVOTEL AM TIERGARTEN
(131 E2) (*ØJ F4*)

Modern, functional hotel at the Tiergarten district line station. Down-to-earth, breezy atmosphere. Attractive sauna area and access for the disabled. A large flea market is held in front of the hotel on Sat and Sun. *274 rooms, 11 suites | Tiergarten | Straße des 17. Juni 106–108 | tel. 030 60 03 50 | www.novotel.com | S Tiergarten*

IBIS BERLIN CITY OST
(145 E5) (*ØJ M4*)

Central location on the banks of the Spree; good value for money, 'non-smoking' floors. *242 rooms | Friedrichshain | An der Schillingbrücke 2 | tel. 030 25 76 00 | www.ibis-berlin.de | S8, 9, 75 Ostbahnhof*

INSIDER TIP ▶ DAS LITERATURHOTEL
(155 F1) (*ØJ G8*)

Books decorate the walls of the breakfast room furnished with antiques. This is also where readings are held. Personal atmosphere. *18 rooms | Friedenau | Fregestr. 68 | tel. 030 8 59 09 60 | www.literaturhotel-berlin.de | S1, 25 Friedenau*

PARK INN BERLIN ALEXANDERPLATZ
(145 D2) (*ØJ L3*)

The 39-storey hotel towers over Alexanderplatz. The rooms have various degrees of comfort. Guests are given vouchers for discounts at the Galeria Kaufhof department store next door. There is a ⚹ INSIDER TIP ▶ viewing platform on the top floor (in summer, from 12noon; in winter

---

MARCO POLO HIGHLIGHTS

HOTELS: BUDGET

from 3pm | 3 euros). *1012 rooms | Mitte | Alexanderplatz 7 | tel. 030 2 38 90 | www.parkinn-Berlin.de | U/S Alexanderplatz*

THE WEINMEISTER (144 C2) *(ᗰ K3)*
A cool designer hotel with a fantastic beauty spa on the 6th floor and ☀ roof terrace. Every room has a Mac Book and a docking station for the iPhone. 24 hour service. *84 rooms | Mitte | Weinmeister-* *str. 2 | tel. 030 75 56 67 46 14 | www.the-weinmeister.com | U 8 Weinmeisterstraße*

HOTELS: BUDGET

FABRIK (146 B5) *(ᗰ N6)*
Ideal for fans of the Kreuzberg nightlife, as they can fall into bed after a night out. Prices start at 18 euros, depending on the size of the room. *45 rooms | Kreuzberg |*

LUXURY HOTELS

Adlon Kempinski
Perfectly presented contemporary interpretation of the luxury hotel on the same site that was destroyed in the war. Impeccable service. *382 rooms, 78 suites | 224–16,000 euros | Mitte | Unter den Linden 77 | tel. 030 2 26 10 | www.hotel-adlon.de | S 1, 2, 25 Brandenburger Tor*

Grand Hyatt
The five star hotel at the Potsdamer Platz is characterized by its simple elegance and modern interior. Highlight is the ☀ wellness landscape on the top floor with a high grade steel pool and best view of the city. *342 rooms and suites | 170–3470 euros | Tiergarten | Marlene-Dietrich-Platz 2 | tel. 030 25 53 12 34 | www.berlin.grand.hyatt.de | U/S Potsdamer Platz*

Hotel Concorde ⭐
Purist, five-star designer hotel with spacious rooms near the memorial church. The 17-floor art-déco-style building was designed by Jan Kleihues. *311 rooms and suites | 130–342 euros | Charlottenburg | Augsburger Str. 41 | tel. 030 8 00 99 90 | www.concorde-hotels.com | U 3, 9 Kurfürstendamm*

Hotel de Rome
Temple of luxury next to the State Opera on Bebelplatz. The rooms and suites are modern with a touch of traditional Berlin architecture. Beautiful rooftop terrace with bar. *146 rooms and suites | 430–4630 euros | Mitte | Behrenstr. 37 | tel. 030 4 60 60 90 | www.hotelderome.com | U 6 Französische Straße*

The Ritz-Carlton Berlin
Top-class hotel, centrally-located at Potsdamer Platz: stately, large spa complex with indoorpool and luxury wherever you look. *303 rooms and suites | 250–14,500 euros | Mitte | Potsdamer Platz 3 | tel. 030 33 77 77 | www.ritzcarlton.com | U/S Potsdamer Platz*

Schlosshotel im Grunewald
Historical palace in a park near Kurfürstendamm. Spa facilities and gourmet restaurant. The interior was designed by Karl Lagerfeld. *53 rooms and suites | 239–5000 euros | Wilmersdorf | Brahmsstr. 10 | tel. 030 89 58 40 | www.schlosshotelberlin.com | S 7, 9 Grünewald*

Sober exterior, classy interior: the Ritz-Carlton on Potsdamer Platz

Schlesische Str. 18 | tel. 030 6118254 | www.diefabrik.com | U 1 Schlesisches Tor

GASTEINER HOF (149 F4) (*⌖ F7*)

Small hotel in the west of the city offering good value for money. Reasonably-priced doubles with shower and WC. *22 rooms | Wilmersdorf | Gasteiner Str. 8 | tel. 030862 0170 | www.gasteiner-hof.de | U 7 Blissestr.*

KARIBUNI (153 F5) (*⌖ N7*)

Family-run hotel in a typical old Berlin building with furniture and wall paintings inspired by Africa. In East Africa, *karibuni* means 'welcome'. *11 rooms, 1 flat | Neukölln | Neckarstraße 2/corner of Karl-Marx-Straße | tel. 030 6 871517 | www.karibuni-hotel.de | U 7 Rathaus Neukölln*

MOTEL ONE
(131 D4) (*⌖ F5*)

Designer hotel with reasonably-priced rooms. Others are located on Alexanderplatz (Mitte), Moritzplatz (Kreuzberg) and near Schloss Bellevue (Tiergarten). *250 rooms | Charlottenburg | Kantstr. 7–11a | tel. 030 31517360 | http://www.motel-one.de | S 7, 9, 75 Zoologischer Garten*

OSTEL
(145 F4) (*⌖ N5*)

With the 'charm' of East Germany for those who find it fun today: the hotel is located in a prefabricated concrete building with original East German furniture and a portrait of Honecker in the lobby. Conveniently situated near the Ostbahnhof. The restaurant even offers original GDR 'cuisine'. *79 rooms, 1 flat | Friedrichshain | Wriezener Karee 5 | tel. 030 25 76 86 60 | www.ostel.eu | S 7, 8, 9 Ostbahnhof*

PETERS
(130 C4) (*⌖ F5*)

Comfortable rooms for non-smokers – and also families – in one of Berlins typical old buildings near Savignyplatz. Many good restaurants in the vicinity. *34 rooms | Charlottenburg | Kantstraße 146 | tel. 030*

Eastern Comfort: let the Spree rock you to sleep

3 12 22 78 | www.pension-peters-berlin.de |
S Savignyplatz

HOSTELS

EASTERN COMFORT
(146 A–B4) (*N5*)
Two small hotel ships along the
Oberbaumbrücke offer you the opportu-
nity to spend a night on the Spree, with
a view through the bulls eye included.
(12–78 euros per night). *42 cabins |
Friedrichshain | Mühlenstr. 73–77 | tel.
030 66 76 38 06 | www.eastern-comfort.
com | U/S Warschauer Straße*

EASTSEVEN (138 C5) (*L2*)
Elected 'Germany's best hostel' in 2009.
The bedrooms are all decorated with mu-
rals and have their own bathrooms (13–37
euros/person in rooms for one to eight
people). *Quiet garden. Prenzlauer Berg |
Schwedter Str. 7 | tel. 030 93 62 22 40 |
www.eastseven.de | U 2 Senefelderplatz*

GENERATOR (0) (*O3*)
Germany's largest hostel with more
than 900 beds soars into the sky near
Landsberger Allee station. Overnight
stays from 15 euros. *241 rooms | Prenzlauer
Berg | Storkower Straße 160 | tel.
030 4 17 24 00 | www.generatorhostels.
com | S 41, 42 Landsberger Allee*

HEART OF GOLD HOSTEL ★
(132 C2) (*K3*)
This is where guests from all over the
world stay in bright, peaceful rooms near
the Oranienburger Straße party zone.
Overnight stays from 10 euros. If you stay
for six nights, the seventh one is free.
*140 rooms | Mitte | Johannisstraße 11 | tel.
030 29 00 33 00 | www.heartofgold-
hostel.de / U 6 Oranienburger Tor*

HÜTTENPALAST (153 E4) (*M7*)
Funny and convenient: camping in a factory hall in Neukölln. Let one of the three
caravans or the three wooden huts harbour you. Nice café and garden terrace.
Additionally an accessibly designed fam-
ily room. *Neukölln | Hobrechtstr. 65–66 |
tel. 030 37 30 58 06 | www.huettenpalast.
de | U 7, 8 Hermannplatz*

THREE LITTLE PIGS (144 A6) (*J5*)
You can stay in two to eight-bed rooms in
a converted monastery near Potsdamer

Platz. Double room with bath: 32 euros/person. *80 rooms | Kreuzberg | Stresemannstr. 66 | tel. 030 32 66 29 55 | www.three-little-pigs.de | U/S Potsdamer Platz*

FLATS

ACKSELHAUS ★
(139 D5) (*ⓜ M2*)

Flats with an Asian touch, a Balinese garden in the courtyard and a goldfish pond. If you stay on the ground floor, you will have to go across stepping stones to reach your entrance. Unbelievably beautiful! *35 rooms | Prenzlauer Berg | Belforter Straße 21 | tel. 030 44 33 76 33 | www.ackselhaus. de | U 2 Senefelderplatz | Expensive*

LUX ELEVEN
(144 C2) (*ⓜ L3*)

Modern-style apartment hotel: bright flats with fully-equipped kitchen including dishwasher and microwave. Ideal for lengthy stays. There is a restaurant with German-Mediterranean cooking in the building. *72 flats | Mitte | Rosa-Luxemburg-Straße 9–13 | tel. 030 9 36 28 00 | www.lux-eleven.com | U 8 Weinmeisterstraße | Expensive*

MINILOFT MITTE ★ ☺
(143 F1) (*ⓜ J3*)

Prize-winning architecture with an impressive glass façade near the main station where you can choose between flats that are classically or extravagantly furnished. Personal, cordial service. Environmentally-friendly operation with eco-electricity and fair-trade products. *14 flats | Mitte | Hessische Str. 5 | tel. 030 8 471090 | www.miniloft. com | U 6 Naturkundemuseum | Moderate*

INSIDER TIPP ▶ PFEFFERBETT
(134 C5) (*ⓜ L2*)

Beautiful dormitories in a former Berlin brewery for two to eight persons *(from 12 euros)*. A double room with your own bathroom, TV and internet access costs approx. 60 euros. *43 beds, 3 app. | Prenzlauer Berg | Christinenstr. 18–19 | tel. 030 93 93 58 58 | www.pfefferbett.de | U 2 Senefelderplatz*

PRIVATE ROOMS

Private rooms and apartments can be booked on the internet under *www. 123berlinzimmer.de* and *www.urban-apartments.com*. There are also various agencies that can arrange shared accommodation including *Freiraum (Kreuzberg) | Wiener Str. 14 | tel. 030 618 20 08 | www.freiraum-berlin.com*.

LOW BUDGET

▶ The *WBM* housing association **(146 C3) (*ⓜ P4*)** *(Scharnweber Str. 23–27 | tel. 030 24 71 53 29 | www. wbm.de | U 5 Samariterstraße)* has ten charming, low-priced apartments in Mitte and Friedrichshain to rent.

▶ The Youth Hostel at Wannsee is a bit far out but idyllically located on the water and also has rooms for families. Overnight stays from 17 euros per person. *Nikolassee* **(0) (*ⓜ 0*)** *(Badeweg 1 | Tel. 030 803 20 34 | www.jh-wannsee.de | S 1, 7 Nikolassee)*

▶ In the *Pension 11. Himmel* **(157 E3) (*ⓜ 0*)** *(5 rooms | Wittenberger Str. 85 | tel. 030 93 77 20 52 | www. pension-11himmel.de | S 7 Ahrensfelde)* in a prefabricated concrete building in Marzahn, you can either sleep in a hammock or a prince's bed. One night with breakfast: 22 euros.

WALKING TOURS

The tours are marked in green in the street atlas, pull-out map and on the back cover

1 WHERE THE WALL ONCE STOOD

You will hardly notice that Berlin was once cut in two by a tremendous amount of cement, barbed wire and minefields. However, there are some places where you can still get an impression of how things were at the time when the city was divided. A walk along the old route of the Wall between Checkpoint Charlie and Friedrichstraße station in Mitte is especially worthwhile.
Duration: around 2 hours

The walk begins at Checkpoint Charlie. Only the small guard house and larger-than-life photographic portraits of Russian and American soldiers remain of what used to be the border crossing for visitors entering East Germany from the west. There is an impressive documentation of escape stories and conditions in the East and West in the Haus am Checkpoint Charlie → p. 52. Until Reunification, 254 people attempting to escape over the Wall were killed by East German border guards. With the stacks of sand sacks behind you, turn left into Zimmerstraße where the Wall originally blocked the view from one side of the street to the other. The corner house is the oldest Baroque building in Friedrichstadt and was erected – originally, with only one storey – in 1735. When you walk down Zimmerstraße you will pass

Stroll through the city where traces of its fascinating past can be felt everywhere

by houses whose occupants used to be almost in the East if they just put their hand out of the window; the Wall was not the actual border, it was a 'virtual' line 2.5 m (8 ft) in front of it! This means that people walking on Zimmerstraße were really in East Berlin. It was forbidden to drive along this street and people living here had to carry everything up to 300 m; this was particularly difficult when someone decided to move. However, tax evaders and criminals were very fond of the address because police and other officials were not allowed to enter East Berlin territory and seizures were subsequently not possible. The East German Ministry for Foreign Trade, with a Stasi (secret police) base and arms cache in the cellar, was located in the building with the brick façade on the other side of the Wall.

Continue across Wilhelmstraße towards the Martin Gropius Building. Here, you will see the last remnants of the almost 4-metre-high (13 ft) Wall constructed of concrete slabs. However, there are a lot of holes in this section because souvenir hunters have hacked out many chunks. Pieces with graffiti were particularly sought-after; in the days when East Germany still existed, the Wall – or at least its West Berlin side – was considered the longest gallery in the world. Hardly any artist of any standing could resist decorating the Wall with a picture. Thierry Noir and Keith Haring were just two of the most famous.

The Topographie des Terrors → p. 53 exhibition centre is located to the left. This used to the headquarters of the Gestapo and SS and a hive of unbelievable fear and horror. There is hardly anywhere else on earth where so much terror, torture and murder was planned and carried out. A new documentation centre on the premises complements the open-air exhibition with 15 sections including one along the remains of the Wall that recalls the fate of the many victims as well as the buildings that once stood here.

Today, the Martin-Gropius-Bau → p. 53, the former Museum of Applied Art that was opened in 1881 and severely damaged in World War II, shows temporary exhibitions on historical, scientific and artistic subjects. It is named after the architect who was a great-uncle of the famous Bauhaus architect Walter Gropius. The Wall made it impossible to use the main entrance and visitors had to go in through the back door. The building in the style of the Italian High Renaissance opposite – on what used to be the east side of the Wall – has housed the Berlin House of Representatives since 1993. It was opened as the Prussian House of Representatives in 1892. The building was also severely damaged in the war and only provisionally renovated by the East Germans and belonged to the neighbouring House of Ministries.

Take a look at the copper inserts in the ground; they mark the former course of the Wall. From Stresemannstraße you can see Potsdamer Platz → p. 45 on the right. New buildings hide where the Wall used to be and only a copper band in the cobblestones along Stresemannstraße recalls the once-divided city.

Where the skyscrapers of the German Federal Railways and Daimler Benz are today, used to be an area of wasteland covering 480,000 square metres (more than 118 acres) when the Wall was still standing. There were only two structures on this site – the Huth wine building and the remains of what was once the fashionable Esplanade Hotel. Until the air-raids in World War II, Potsdamer Platz was the busiest place in Europe and was also the site of Berlin's first traffic lights that were installed in 1925. This is commemorated by a tower with a clock and horizontal set of lights at the entrance to the station. The gigantic tent roof of the Sony Center → p. 45 is flooded with coloured light emitted by thousands of LEDs after night falls. If you have enough time, visit the Film Museum Berlin → p. 43 here or have some fried chicken on the terrace of the Lindenbräu brewery with a fine view into the circle of this impressive building designed by Helmut Jahn. Billy Wilder's bar → p. 87 directly on Potsdamer Straße is also a perfect place to take a rest in the evening and try one of its many cocktails and varieties of vodka.

Continue along Ebertstraße towards Pariser Platz. The so-called Ministergärten (Minister Gardens) with the representations of numerous federal states lie on the right. This is adjacent to the Denkmal für die ermordeten Juden Europas → p. 42 based on plans by the New York architect Peter Eisenman. When you reach Brandenburg Gate → p. 41, you should take a break and visit the INSIDER TIP Raum der Stille (Room of Silence). It is located in the northern column of the gate and is the right place to rest your tired feet. It is hard to believe that only 23 years ago nobody was allowed to pass through Brandenburg Gate because it was in no-man's-land between East and West. Two million people took part in the first joint New Year's celebration held around the gate

around the Reichstag is considered an ecologically-exemplary ensemble of buildings heated used rapeseed oil and solar energy. The rays of sun flowing in through the glass dome are channelled downwards using mirrors to provide the parliament chamber beneath with natural light. A ground-water storage system also supplies the government buildings with energy.

A field of steles you can walk around: the Denkmal für die ermordeten Juden Europas

in 1989/90. The buildings to the north of Brandenburg Gate are new even though they do not look it. The best place to go if you feel like having a cup of coffee or something small to eat is Theodor Tucher Café → p. 69. A gallery with many books will tempt you to browse a bit and you can enjoy relaxing in the comfortable chairs. Rejuvenated, head off to the Reichstag building → p. 47 today the seat of the Lower House of the German Parliament. Visitors to its ⚘ dome have a fantastic view over the centre of Berlin. The government district

The Wall used to run behind the parliament building on the Spree side. The memorial site 'Parliament of Trees against War and Violence', conceived by the Berlin environmental artist Ben Wargin in 1990, is located opposite the Reichstag, behind Elisabeth-Lüders-House. It consists of segments of the Wall as well as trees arranged in squares. Take the path along the riverbank past the ARD-Hauptstadt-studio (ARD Television's Berlin Studio). If you are interested, take a free guided tour (Wed, Sat 3pm) through the television and sound studios and find out how news programmes are produced *(Mitte | Wilhelmstraße 67a | tel. 030 22 88 11 10 | www.ardhauptstadtstudio.de).* It is now only stone's throw to **Friedrichstraße Station**; just go along the Spree to the east and you will reach it in five minutes. Maybe you'd like to do some shopping? There is plenty of choice on **Friedrichstraße** with its many fashion and trendy shops and the **Dussmann → p. 81** 'culture department store'. If you want to see more of the city, take one of the excursion steamers that dock at Friedrichstraße station and chug through the centre of Berlin to the Museumsinsel.

2 THROUGH BERLIN'S HISTORY: SPANDAUER VORSTADT

The name says it all: in the 18th century, new housing was needed and the city expanded into an area that became known as the Spandauer Vorstadt – 'suburban Spandau' beyond the city walls as the road to Spandau started outside the city perimeter. Today, many media agencies, fashionable boutiques and bars have set up business here. Duration: around one hour

The Scheunenviertel ('barn district'), part of Spandauer Vorstadt today, is located to the north of the Hackescher Mark district line station. In the 18th century there was a row of barns here lined up like pearls on a necklace. This was intended to prevent fire from spreading within the city's limits. At the time, Spandauer Vorstadt was mainly an agricultural and trading centre but urban life gradually developed. The 'golden 20s' saw things flourish in the fields of culture and crafts. People of various religions including many Jews – mainly from Eastern Europe – lived in the Scheunenviertel. Today this suburb is once again seeing a resurgence of this tradition

as a centre of the theatre, arts and crafts, together a variety of shops and cafes.

The **Hackescher Markt district line station**, where our walk begins, marks the former border of the city; regional and long-distance trains travel above the foundations of the old city wall between Jannowitzbrücke and Friedrichstraße. The district line station is named after the City Commandant von Hacke who had the swampland drained in the middle of the 18th century. The **Hackesche Höfe → p. 37** opposite the square in front of the station are also named after him. The eight courtyards, one behind each other, form Europe's largest complex of this kind and now offer a great variety of fashion, culture, arts and crafts, and restaurants. If you wall through the courtyards you will reach **INSIDER TIP** Sophienstraße – a spruced-up street that the political leaders of East Berlin ordered to be renovated in the 1980s for the 750th anniversary of the city. At the same time, just a few blocks away, Spandauer Vorstadt was allowed to go to rack and ruin. Going to the left, you will pass the old churchyard of the **Sophienkirche** with the oldest Baroque church tower in the city. The **Handwerkervereinshaus** (House of the Arts and Crafts Association) is on the right. Built in 1844, the gathering place of Berlin's first labour organisation. As many as 3000 people held meetings and had discussions inside. In the 1920s in particular, Communists, Social Democrats and National Socialists held their party meetings here. So-called 'ring societies', mafia-like gangs of criminals, also met there regularly.

A few yards further on, the route leads us through a gateway into the **Sophie-Gips-Höfe** where multi-media companies, galleries and gastronomic businesses have opened up. Art lovers are particularly fond of the **Sammlung Hoffmann**, a private collection of contemporary art, that is open to the public on Sat *(to book: tel. 030 28 49 91 21)*. The American cakes in Barcomi's Café are delicious and in sum-

Hospital on the right. It was opened as a hospital for the old and infirm in 1888 and is dedicated to Saint Hedwig who was

A peaceful place: Sophie-Gips-Höfe in Spandauer Vorstadt

mer you can sit in bliss on the courtyard terrace. The rear exit of the courtyard ensemble leads to **Gipsstraße** ('plaster street'). This is one of Spandauer Vorstadt's oldest streets. There used to be a lime kiln in the street for the production of plaster – hence the name. Go along the street on the left to the end. The 19th century 'Gründerzeit' houses have now been renovated and it is worth taking a look into the courtyards that often still have single-storey barns.

You will now have reached Auguststraße; after around 50 metres, turn to the left onto **Große Hamburger Straße**. In the 1920s it was famous as a place where Jews, Protestants and Catholics lived together peacefully. You will soon see the pretty clinker brick façade of **St Hedwig**

famous for caring for the poor and ill during the Christianisation of Silesia in the 12th century. The Jewish school is at Große Hamburger Straße 27. There used to be a Jewish cemetery next to the schoolyard but it was turned into a park for the former Jewish old people's home in 1827. The SS organised deportations to concentration camps from this home that no longer stands today. A memorial stone and sculpture reminds us of the 56,000 Berlin Jews who were deported to Nazi death camps. **House number 19a**, opposite the former cemetery, is thought to be the oldest in Spandauer Vorstadt. Turn left onto Oranienburger Straße at the end of the street. After around 100 metres, you will once again see the Hackescher Markt where our tour ends.

TRAVEL WITH KIDS

`INSIDER TIP` **BONBONMACHEREI**
(132–133 C–D2) *(🕮 K3)*

How are sweets made? Kids can see how the mixture is prepared and also try them while still warm. Of course, you can also buy the drops packed up in little bags. Yummy! *Wed–Sat 12noon–8pm | entrance free | closed July/August and over Christmas/New Year | Mitte | Oranienburger Str. 32 | tel. 030 44 05 52 43 | www.bonbonmacherei.de | S 1, 2, 25 Oranienburger Straße*

`INSIDER TIP` **BVG CABRIOTOUR**
(133 F2) *(🕮 L3)*

A 'ghost train' ride in the underground: during the summer season, a roofless carriage races through 35 km (22 miles) of dark tunnels in the underground system. Ready, set, helmets on – for the two hour tour starting at the Alexanderplatz. *April–Oct, every second Fri 7 and 10.20pm | tickets 40 euros, children 25 euros | tel. 030 25 62 52 56 | www.bvg.de | U/S Alexanderplatz*

KINDERBAD MONBIJOU
(133 D2) *(🕮 K3)*

A lovely pool only for children with their parents or accompanying adult. The water is not deeper than 1.3 m (4 ft 3 in.) and parents quickly make contact with others at the water's edge. Nobody over the age of 15 is allowed in unless they are accompanied by a child. *June–Sept, Mon–Fri 11am–7pm, Sat/Sun 10am–7pm | entrance fee 4 euros | Mitte | Oranienburger Str. 78 | tel. 030 2 82 86 52 | www.berlinerbaeder betriebe.de | S 1, 2, 25 Oranienburger Str.*

KINDERINSEL
(144 A1) *(🕮 K3)*

You want to place your children in good care and go out on your own? They will be well looked-after here; by the hour or even overnight. Qualified personnel and a bright, friendly atmosphere guarantee a lot of fun. Children from 6 months to 14 years of age are cared for. *Daily | 13 euros/hour, 69 euros/night, 50 per cent discount for siblings | Mitte | Eichendorffstr. 17 | tel. 030 41 71 69 28 | www.kinderinsel.de | U 6 Naturkundemuseum*

KULTURPROJEKTE BERLIN

Most of the state museums have regular guided tours for children and workshops on the art on display. Just one example; in the Music Instrument Museum, the way instruments function is investigated

Children love big cities because there is so much to discover. And there is a great deal waiting for them in Berlin. Enjoy yourselves!

playfully using the work 'Peter and the Wolf' by Sergei Prokofiev. The staff have all studied art history or are trained teachers and have no difficulties in making young people really enthusiastic about museums. You can find details of current events by phone. *Office: Mon–Fri 9am–4pm, Sat/Sun 9am–1pm | Mitte | Klosterstr. 68 | tel. 030 24 74 98 88 | www.kulturprojekte-berlin.de | U 2 Klosterstraße*

LOXX (145 D3) (*M L4*)

One of the world's largest digitally-controlled model railways will make children's hearts beat faster. Intercity expresses, regional and local trains travel over 4 km (2.5 mi) of tracks through a Berlin-style cityscape with the Brandenburg Gate, an airport and a sea of houses. *Daily | 10am–8pm | entrance fee 12 euros; concessions 7 euros | Mitte | Grunerstr. 20 in the Alexa Shopping Centre | www.loxx-berlin.de | U/S Alexanderplatz*

MACH MIT! MUSEUM (139 E3) (*M M2*)

Shelves you can climb on, soap shops, a crawling area – there are a lot of unusual things in the Museum for children and you can try many of them out. There are workshops for handicrafts, pottery and acting. Exhibitions are also shown – on salt, for example. You can park your parents in the Family Café while you have fun! *Tue–Sun 10am–6pm | entrance fee 4.50 euros; concessions 3 euros | Prenzlauer Berg | Senefelderstraße 5 | tel. 030 74 77 82 00 | www.machmitmuseum.de | S 41, Prenzlauer Allee*

THEATER AN DER PARKAUE (147 D2) (*M P4*)

Theatre for children and youngsters. Oscar Wilde's 'Canterville Ghost' is a hit with children from the age of eight. 'The Children's Transport – Berlin Kids on the Way to London' has even won prizes. *Lichtenberg | Parkaue 29 | tel. 030 5 57 75 20 | www.parkaue.de | S 41, 42 Frankfurter Allee*

FESTIVALS & EVENTS

Numerous events are real crowd-pullers. These include the 'Long Night of the Museums' that is held twice a year and gets thousand up and about. Shuttle buses transport visitors from one museum to the next and – in spite of all the crowding – everyone has a good time. In any case, the people of Berlin like to do things in big groups. Whether it's the Carnival or Christopher Street Day, the motto is always 'the more, the merrier'!

SPECIAL EVENTS

JANUARY/FEBRUARY
▶ *Sechstagerennen* (Six-day race): High-spirited bicycle race in the Velodrom; *Prenzlauer Berg | Landsberger Allee | tel. 030 44 30 44 30 | www.sechstagerennen-berlin.de*
▶ *Grüne Woche:* Delicatessen specialities from all over the world at the Funkturm (Radio Tower); *Charlottenburg | info tel. 030 3 03 80 | www.gruenewoche.de*
▶ *Lange Nacht der Museen* (Long Night of the Museums): Evening visit to van Gogh & co; *info tel.: 030 24 74 98 88 | www.lange-nacht-der-museen.de*

FEBRUARY
▶ ⭐ *Berlinale:* International film festival; ten days of razzmatazz with German and international film stars and new cinema productions; *info tel. 030 25 92 00 | www.berlinale.de*

MARCH
▶ *Internationale Tourismusbörse (ITB):* International Tourism Fair at the Funkturm; *Charlottenburg | tel. 030 3 03 80 | www.itb-berlin.de*

MAY/JUNE
▶ *Internationale Luft- und Raumfahrtausstellung:* Every two years, Schönefeld Airport is the place to be for all aviation enthusiasts (next fairs: 2016); *www.ila-berlin.de*
▶ *DFB Cup Final:* Football festival in the Olympia Stadium; *Charlottenburg | info tel. 030 8 96 99 40*
▶ *Karneval der Kulturen:* Colourful, inter-cultural carnival procession on Whit Sunday; *www.karneval-der-kulturen.de*
▶ *Theatertreffen* inspirational get-together for theatre fans; *info tel. 030 25 48 92 33 | www.berlinerfestspiele.de/theatertreffen*

Not only in summer is Berlin a city where people like to have a good time – the calendar is full of festivals of all kinds

JUNE/JULY

▶ *Christopher Street Day:* Top event for gays and lesbians with a great parade from Kreuzberg to Brandenburg Gate; *www.csd.berlin.de*

▶ **Lange Nacht der Wissenschaften**: Presentation of work at research institutions; *www.langenachtderwissenschaften.de*

▶ *Classic Open Air on Gendarmenmarkt:* Festive setting, catchy tunes; *Mitte | tel. 01805 9 69 00 06 06 (*) | www.classicopenair.de*

AUGUST

Second ▶ *Long Night of the Museums*

SEPTEMBER

▶ *Berlin Festival:* Pop, electro and techno at Tempelhof Airport; *www.berlinfestival.de*

▶ *Internationale Funkausstellung:* Entertainment/electronics fair at the Funkturm; *Charlottenburg | b2c.ifa-berlin.de*

▶ *Berlin Marathon:* More than 40,000 participants from all over the world start at Brandenburg Gate; *info tel. 030 30 12 88 10 | www.berlin-marathon.com*

▶ *Musikfest Berlin:* Classical music of the highest standard; *www.berlinerfestspiele.de*

▶ *Jüdische Kulturtage* (Jewish Culture Days): Theatre performances, concerts and readings; *www.juedische-kulturtage.org*

SEPTEMBER/OCTOBER

▶ *Internationales Literaturfestival:* Numerous discussions with authors and readings; *www.literaturfestival.com*

▶ *Festival of Lights:* After nightfall, installations cast many of Berlin's sights in a new light; *festival-of-lights.de*

NOVEMBER

▶ *Jazzfest Berlin:* An institution with international stars in the field; *info tel. 030 25 48 91 00 | www.jazzfest-berlin.de*

DECEMBER

▶ *Weihnachtsmarkt am Gendarmenmarkt:* the most beautiful – offering artisan craftwork and concerts

LINKS, BLOGS, APPS & MORE

LINKS

▶ www.berlin.de/international is Berlin's official internet site that offers comprehensive listings for hotels, entertainment, tickets for local events well as practical information about local authorities and online maps

▶ www.tourist.visitberlin.de is an informative site with interesting offers for tourists to Berlin; including a list of events and travel tips for various age groups along with some useful listings for special interest groups like for example the environmentally aware

▶ www.exberliner.com Berlin's online English language magazine which includes listings for cultural events, reviews, general interest articles and a large classified section. The title is a play on expat

VIDEOS, STREETART & PODCASTS

▶ On www.youtube.com there is an excellent 2009 seven minute video by the Berlin Tourist Board

▶ www.myvideo.de/Videos_A-Z?searchWord=berlin if you search for 'Berlin' on MyVideo you will not only find many TV series but also documentaries and whimsical short films

▶ www.art-in-berlin.de/video.php Video documentary reports about current exhibitions and the corresponding artists

▶ https://itunes.apple.com/us/podcast/berlin-stories-podcast/id302399493?mt=2 These podcasts are from the bi-weekly English radio broadcasts of 104.1 fm NPR Berlin. American and British writers read their reflections on Berlin and there also special editions with readings of passages from historical novels about B

Regardless of whether you are still preparing your trip or already in Berlin: these addresses will provide you with more information, videos and networks to make your holiday even more enjoyable.

▶ www.thewednesdaychef.com/berlin_on_a_platter/ an excellent and informative foodie blog written by the cookbook editor and award winning blogger Luisa Weiss. She writes about her 'favourite bakeries and snack stands, hidden gems, gustatory wonders' and new restaurant discoveries

▶ http://www.digitalinberlin.de is a site that is perfect for 'music lovers, adventures and individualists' with listings for music, movies, literature, interviews and free downloads

▶ www.toytowngermany.com is the best online forum for expats in Germany and the topics of discussion include local news, reviews, relocation issues as well as legal and financial advice. The forum also organises a number of live social events via the site

▶ Berlin Unlike City Guide is an app by a team of fashion, art and music professionals who recommend the highlights of Berlin with constantly updated listing and events and punchy reviews

▶ Fahrinfo Berlin is an important companion in public transport: with a planner that shows the quickest way to get from A to B and time table listing for all the public transport route networks in Berlin

▶ Spotted by Locals is an app that will allow you to experience Berlin 'like a local' and contains regularly updated tips by handpicked passionate Berlin locals.

▶ www.travelpod.com/s/berlin?st=user First-hand reports, travel blogs, photos and even short videos by international Berlin tourists

▶ www.phone-guide-germany.com/free-wifi-hotspots-berlin A great site that has a comprehensive list of free wifi hotspots

TRAVEL TIPS

ARRIVAL

✈ Tempelhof Airport has been closed and now visitors arriving by air land at one of the other two airports. Most planes land and take off from Tegel Airport in the north-west of the city. You can reach Bahnhof Zoo in about 20 min by taking the buses X9 and 109. To reach Alexanderplatz (in about 30 min, via Unter den Linden) take the express bus TXL. Mostly charters and flights from and to East Europe use Schönefeld Airport. From here, take the S 9 to Alexanderplatz (35 min) or to Bahnhof Zoo (50 min). *Airport information: tel. 030 60 91 11 50 | www.berlin-airport.de*

🚃 The most convenient way to travel is using the railway. There are fast train connections (ICE and IC) from major European stations to Berlin-Spandau, Main Station and East Station. *Information: tel. 0800 150 70 90 | www.bahn.de*

RESPONSIBLE TRAVEL

While traveling you can influence a lot. Don't just keep track of your carbon footprint *(www.myclimate.org)* by planning an ecologically harmless route. Also think about how you can protect nature and culture abroad *(www.ecotrans.org)*. It is all the more important that as a tourist you take into consideration aspects such as the conservation of nature *(www.wwf.org)*, regional products, minimal use of cars, saving water and many more things. For more information on ecological Tourism look at *www.ecotourism.org*.

🚗 The motorways to and from Berlin are good. However, there are often traffic jams on the Stadtring (A10) ring road. The city centre within the inner district line ring is a 'green zone'; only cars with a green sticker are allowed to drive here. *www.umwelt-plakette.de*

🚌 There are regular bus services several times a week from all German and many foreign towns to Berlin. Berlin's Central Bus Station is located in Charlottenburg opposite the Funkturm. *Info tel. 030 86 09 62 11 | www.berlinlinienbus.de*

ADVANCE SALES

For those who make up their mind at the last minute; *HEKticket* sells remaining tickets at half-price until shortly before performances begin. INSIDER TIP Tickets for museums (incl. *Madame Tussauds*) are also available at reduced prices *(Hardenbergstraße 29d | tel. 030 2 30 99 30 | www.hekticket.de)*.

Showtime-Konzert- und Theaterkassen sell tickets in the branches of Karstadt and KaDeWe department stores. *Tel. 030 80 60 29 29 | www.showtimetickets.de*

BANKS

Normal opening hours are 10am to 5pm on weekdays; some banks however are open until 2pm on Saturdays.
Telephone numbers to block lost mobile phones, bank and credit cards
– *Amex, EC, Eurocard, VISA, mobile phone: tel. 11 61 16*
– *Diners Club: tel. 01805 07 07 04 (*)*

From arrival to weather

Holiday from start to finish: the most important addresses and information for your Berlin trip

BICYCLES & VELOTAXIS

You can rent a bicycle from many bike points in the city centre. The German Railway's (DB) 'Call a Bike' is very practical. The conspicuous DB bikes can be found at 50 different places in the heart of Berlin. They can be rented directly at a terminal, by telephone or app using your bank card or credit card. New clients have to register first. To begin with, 7.50 euros are booked from your account as credit. Fees are 8 cents/minute rising to a maximum of 12 euros/day.

Those who find this too strenuous can rent a Biketaxi and have somebody else do the hard work. A 60-minute tour with an individual route costs 45 euros. *Bookings: tel. 030 93 95 83 46 | www.biketaxi.de.* Or just stop an empty rickshaw on the street. The first kilometre costs 6 euros; after that, there is an hourly rate.

CITY TOURS

Bus no. 100 is terrific for those who like to get an overview on their own. It runs from Bahnhof Zoo to Alexanderplatz and is ideal for sightseeing – you pass most of the important attractions in the centre.

BERLINER UNTERWELTEN

Exciting tours below or above ground include a bunker tour through the flak (anti-aircraft gun blockhouse) tower in the Humboldthain Volkspark: *tel. 030 49 91 05 17 | www.berliner-unterwelten.de | 10 euros | U/S Gesundbrunnen*

BEROLINA SIGHTSEEING

City-Circle-Tour with 20 stops to hop on or off; the buses depart every 10 minutes

BUDGETING

Coffee	2–3 euros a cup of coffee
Ice cream	2 euros for two scoops of ice cream
Döner	2.50–3 euros for a döner kebab
Museum	4–12 euros entrance to state-run museums
Bus	2.30 euros for a bus ticket

(10am– 6pm) in summer. Day ticket 22 euros; half-day 16.50 euros; start: Kurfürstendamm/Meinekestraße. *Info tel. 030 88 56 80 30 | www.berolina-Berlin.com*

INSIDER TIP ▶ ROUTE 44

Migrant women guide visitors through the Neukölln district around Richardplatz. Those taking part find out how the women and girls live here. Incl. visit to a mosque. *Kulturbewegt e.V. | 3 euros | tel. 030 70 22 20 23 | www.route44-neukoelln.de*

SOLAR BOAT TOUR ☺

With the four-hour circular tour on the solar boat you will see many places and buildings and save energy at the same time. Starting and finishing point: Urbanhafen in Kreuzberg. *tel. 0151 54 22 80 44 | www.solarpolis.de*

INSIDER TIP ▶ TOURS OF THE WALL BY TAXI ●

Two-hour personal tour with stops at historically-important sites. Price: 60

euros for one person; 10 euros for each additional passenger. *tel. 0160 95 32 80 52 | www.taxi-wall-fahrten.de*

CUSTOMS

EU citizens may import and export goods for their personal use tax-free (800 cigarettes, 90 l of wine). Duty-free for non-EU citizens are: 50g perfume, 2 l of wine, 1 l of spirits and 200 cigarettes.

EMBASSSIES & CONSULATES

BRITISH EMBASSY
Wilhelmstraße 70 | 10117 Berlin | tel. 030 20457 0 | www.ukingermany.fco.gov.uk

CURRENCY CONVERTER

£	€	€	£
1	1.20	1	0.80
3	3.70	3	2.50
5	6.10	5	4.10
13	15.90	13	10.60
40	48.90	40	32.70
75	92	75	61
120	147	120	98
250	306	250	204
500	611	500	409

$	€	€	$
1	0.70	1	1.40
3	2.20	3	4.10
5	3.60	5	6.90
13	9.50	13	17.80
40	29.10	40	54.90
75	55	75	103
120	87	120	165
250	182	250	343
500	364	500	686

For current exchange rates see www.xe.com

EMBASSY OF THE UNITED STATES
Clayallee 170 | 14191 Berlin | tel. 030 83 05 0 | www.germany.usembassy.gov

EMBASSY OF CANADA
Leipziger Platz 17 | 10117 Berlin | tel. 030 20 312 0 | www.canadainternational.gc.ca/ germany-allemagne/contact-contactez

EMERGENCY SERVICES

On-call medical service: 030 31 00 31 | Drug emergency service: 030 192 37 | Fire brigade: tel. 112 | Police: tel. 110 | On-call dentist: tel. 030 89 00 43 33

IMMIGRATION

No visa is necessary for EU citizens to travel to or work in Germany. Non-EU citizens require a visa (valid up to 90 days) – or a residence or settlement permit. More detailed, up-to-date information available online, e.g. *www.workpermit.com/germany/employer1.htm.*

INFORMATION

BERLIN TOURISMUS MARKETING GMBH
Karlsbad 11 | 10785 Berlin | tel. 030 25 00 25 | www.visitberlin.de | Mon–Fri 9am–7pm, Sat 10am–6pm, Sun 10am–2pm
Branches:
– Mitte | Pariser Platz (Brandenburg Gate, south wing) | daily 9.30am–7pm
– Mitte | Grunerstr. 20 (in the Alexa Shopping Centre) | Mon–Sat 10am–10pm
– Mitte | Europaplatz 1 | main railway station | daily 8am–8pm
– Charlottenburg | Kranzler-Eck (Kurfürstendamm Passage) | Mon–Sat 9.30am–8pm; Sun 9.30am–6pm
– Mitte | Humboldtbox | Unter den Linden (Schlossplatz) | daily 10am–6pm

PHONE & MOBILE PHONE

The international dialling code for Germany is 0049, the area code for Berlin is (0)30. Dial 0044 for Great Britain followed by the area code without '0' and 001 for USA and Canada. There are four main providers in Germany: T-Mobile (D1), Vodafone (D2), E-Plus (coverage of the E-Net is not as good as D-Net) and O2. Germany operates on a GSM network.

Currently, a single ticket (A) costs 2.30 euros (concessions: 1.40 euros); day ticket 6.30 euros. *BVG Information: tel. 030 19 49 | www.bvg.de*

Families can travel economically with the Welcome Card available in the BTM Online Shop under *www.visitberlin.de*, where tickets for the district line, BVG, and DB Regio are sold, as well as at the information centres run by Berlin Tourismus Marketing and in many hotels.

PUBLIC TRANSPORT

Most underground lines run around the clock on Fri and Sat – all through the night. If there is no underground to where you are staying, night buses will bring you back to your accommodation. The district line usually runs until around 1am. There are three fare zones for suburban services. A and B cover the whole city; C also covers the surrounding area including Potsdam.

TAXI

The basic fare is 3.20 euros, normal fare for distances of up to 7 km (just less than 4½ miles) 1.65 euros/km; from 7 km, 1.28 euros/km. Short distances under 2 km (1¼ miles) that do not take longer than 10 minutes cost 4 euros/journey. These fares only apply to taxis that are flagged down. You must ask for them. *www.taxi-in-berlin.de/taxitarif*

WEATHER IN BERLIN

	Jan	Feb	March	April	May	June	July	Aug	Sept	Oct	Nov	Dec
Daytime temperatures in °C/°F	2/36	3/37	8/46	13/55	19/66	22/72	24/75	23/73	19/66	13/55	7/45	3/37
Nighttime temperatures in °C/°F	−3/27	−3/27	0/32	4/39	8/46	12/54	14/57	13/55	10/50	6/43	2/36	−1/30
Sunshine hours/day	2	3	5	6	8	8	8	7	6	4	2	1
Precipitation days/month	11	9	8	9	9	9	11	9	8	9	10	9

USEFUL PHRASES GERMAN

PRONUNCIATION

We have provided a simple pronunciation aid for the german words
(see the square brackets). Note the following:

ch   usually like ch in Scottish "loch", shown here as [kh]
g   hard as in "get"
ß   is a double s
ä   like the vowel in "fair" or "bear"
ö   a little like er as in "her"
ü   is spoken as ee with rounded lips, like the French "tu"
ie   is ee as in "fee", but ei is like "height", shown here as [ei]
'   stress on the following syllable

IN BRIEF

Yes/No/Maybe	Ja [yah]/Nein [nein]/Vielleicht [fee'leikht]
Please/Thank you	Bitte ['bi-te]/Danke ['dan-ke]
Sorry	Entschuldige [ent'shul-di-ge]
Excuse me, please	Entschuldigen Sie [ent'shul-di-gen zee]
May I ...?/ Pardon?	Darf ich ...? [darf ikh]/Wie bitte? [vee 'bi-te]
I would like to .../	Ich möchte ... [ikh 'merkh-te]/
have you got ...?	Haben Sie ...? ['hab-en zee]
How much is ...?	Wie viel kostet ...? [vee-feel 'koss-tet]
I (don't) like this	Das gefällt mir/nicht [das ge-'felt meer/nikht]
good/bad	gut/schlecht [goot/shlekht]
broken/doesn't work	kaputt [ka-'put]/funktioniert nicht/
	funk-tsion-'eert nikht]
too much/much/little	(zu) viel/wenig [tsoo feel/'vay-nikh]
Help!/Attention!/ Caution!	Hilfe! ['hil-fe]/Achtung! [akh-'tung]/ Vorsicht! ['for-sikht]
ambulance	Krankenwagen ['kran-ken-vaa-gen]/
	Notarzt ['note-aatst]
police/fire brigade	Polizei [pol-i-'tsei]/Feuerwehr ['foy-er-vayr]
danger/dangerous	Gefahr [ge-'far]/gefährlich [ge-'fair-likh]

GREETINGS, FAREWELL

Good morning!/after- noon!/evening!/night!	Gute(n) Morgen ['goo-ten 'mor-gen]/Tag [taag]/ Abend ['aa-bent]/Nacht [nakht]
Hello!/Goodbye!	Hallo ['ha-llo]/Auf Wiedersehen [owf 'vee-der-zayn]

Sprechen Sie Deutsch?

"Do you speak German?" This guide will help you to say the basic words and phrases in German.

See you!	Tschüss [chüss]
My name is ...	Ich heiße ... [ikh 'hei-sse]
What's your name?	Wie heißt Du [vee heist doo]/ heißen Sie? ['heiss-en zee]
I'm from ...	Ich komme aus ... [ikh 'ko-mme ows]

DATE & TIME

Monday/Tuesday	Montag ['moan-tag]/Dienstag ['deens-tag]
Wednesday/Thursday	Mittwoch ['mit-vokh]/Donnerstag ['don-ers-tag]
Friday/Saturday	Freitag ['frei-tag]/Samstag ['zams-tag]
Sunday/holiday	Sonntag ['zon-tag]/Feiertag ['fire-tag]
today/tomorrow/ yesterday	heute ['hoy-te]/morgen ['mor-gen]/ gestern ['gess-tern]
hour/minute	Stunde ['shtun-de]/Minute [min-'oo-te]
day/night/week	Tag [tag]/Nacht [nakht]/Woche ['vo-khe]
What time is it?	Wie viel Uhr ist es? ['vee-feel oor ist es]
It's three o'clock	Es ist drei Uhr [ez ist drei oor]

TRAVEL

open/closed	offen ['off-en]/geschlossen [ge-'shloss-en]
entrance (vehicles)	Zufahrt ['tsoo-faat]
entrance/exit	Eingang ['ein-gang]/Ausgang ['ows-gang]
arrival/arrival (flight)	Ankunft ['an-kunft]/Abflug ['ap-floog]
toilets/restrooms / ladies/gentlemen	Toiletten [twa-'let-en]/ Damen ['daa-men]/Herren ['her-en]
(no) drinking water	(kein) Trinkwasser [(kein) 'trink-vass-er]
Where is ...?/Where are ...?	Wo ist ...? [vo ist]/Wo sind ...? [vo zint]
left/right	links [links]/rechts [rekhts]
straight ahead/back	geradeaus [ge-raa-de-'ows]/zurück [tsoo-'rük]
close/far	nah [naa]/weit [veit]
taxi/cab	Taxi ['tak-si]
bus stop/ cab stand	Bushaltestelle [bus-hal-te-'shtell-e]/ Taxistand ['tak-si- shtant]
parking lot/parking garage	Parkplatz ['park-plats]/Parkhaus ['park-hows]
street map/map	Stadtplan ['shtat-plan]/Landkarte ['lant-kaa-te]
airport/ train station	Flughafen ['floog-ha-fen]/ Bahnhof ['baan-hoaf]
schedule/ticket	Fahrplan ['faa-plan]/Fahrschein ['faa-shein]
I would like to rent ...	Ich möchte ... mieten [ikh 'mer-khte ... 'mee-ten]
a car/a bicycle	ein Auto [ein 'ow-to]/ein Fahrrad [ein 'faa-raat]
a motorhome/RV	ein Wohnmobil [ein 'vone-mo-beel]
a boat	ein Boot [ein 'boat]

petrol/gas station	Tankstelle ['tank-shtell-e]
petrol/gas / diesel	Benzin [ben-'tseen]/Diesel ['dee-zel]
breakdown/repair shop	Panne ['pan-e]/Werkstatt ['verk-shtat]

FOOD & DRINK

Could you please book a table for tonight for four?	Reservieren Sie uns bitte für heute Abend einen Tisch für vier Personen [rez-er-'vee-ren zee uns 'bi-te für 'hoy-te 'aa-bent 'ein-en tish für feer pair-'zo-nen]
The menu, please	Die Speisekarte, bitte [dee 'shpei-ze-kaa-te 'bi-te]
Could I please have ...?	Könnte ich ... haben? ['kern-te ikh ... 'haa-ben]
with/without ice/sparkling	mit [mit]/ohne Eis ['oh-ne eis]/Kohlensäure ['koh-len-zoy-re]
vegetarian/allergy	Vegetarier(in) [veg-e-'taa-ree-er]/Allergie [al-air-'gee]
May I have the bill, lease?	Ich möchte zahlen, bitte [ikh 'merkh-te 'tsaa-len 'bi-te]

SHOPPING

Where can I find...?	Wo finde ich ...? [vo 'fin-de ikh]
I'd like .../I'm looking for ...	Ich möchte ... [ikh 'merkh-te]/Ich suche ... [ikh 'zoo-khe]
pharmacy/chemist	Apotheke [a-po-'tay-ke]/Drogerie [dro-ge-'ree]
shopping centre	Einkaufszentrum [ein-kowfs-'tsen-trum]
expensive/cheap/price	teuer ['toy-er]/billig ['bil-ig]/Preis [preis]
more/less	mehr [mayr]/weniger ['vay-ni-ger]
organically grown	aus biologischem Anbau [ows bee-o-'lo-gish-em 'an-bow]

WHERE TO STAY

I have booked a room	Ich habe ein Zimmer reserviert [ikh 'haa-be ein 'tsi-me rez-erv-'eert]
Do you have any ... left?	Haben Sie noch ein ... ['haa-ben zee nokh]
single room	Einzelzimmer ['ein-tsel-tsi-mer]
double room	Doppelzimmer ['dop-el-tsi-mer]
breakfast/half board	Frühstück ['frü-shtük]/Halbpension ['halp-pen-si-ohn]
full board	Vollpension ['foll-pen-si-ohn]
shower/sit-down bath	Dusche ['doo-she]/Bad [baat]
balcony/terrace	Balkon [bal-'kohn]/Terrasse [te-'rass-e]
key/room card	Schlüssel ['shlü-sel]/Zimmerkarte ['tsi-mer-kaa-te]
luggage/suitcase	Gepäck [ge-'pek]/Koffer ['koff-er]/Tasche ['ta-she]

BANKS, MONEY & CREDIT CARDS

bank/ATM	Bank/Geldautomat [bank/'gelt-ow-to-maat]
pin code	Geheimzahl [ge-'heim-tsaal]
I'd like to change ... euros	Ich möchte ... Euro wechseln [ikh 'merkh-te ... 'oy-ro 'vek-seln]

| cash/credit card | bar [bar]/Kreditkarte [kre-'dit-kaa-te] |
| bill/coin | Banknote ['bank-noh-te]/Münze ['mün-tse] |

HEALTH

doctor/dentist/ paediatrician	Arzt [aatst]/Zahnarzt ['tsaan-aatst]/ Kinderarzt ['kin-der-aatst]
hospital/ emergency clinic	Krankenhaus ['kran-ken-hows]/ Notfallpraxis ['note-fal-prak-sis]
fever/pain	Fieber ['fee-ber]/Schmerzen ['shmer-tsen]
diarrhoea/nausea	Durchfall ['doorkh-fal]/Übelkeit ['ü-bel-keit]
inflamed/injured	entzündet [ent-'tsün-det]/verletzt [fer-'letst]
prescription	Rezept [re-'tsept]
pain reliever/tablet	Schmerzmittel ['shmerts-mit-el]/Tablette [ta-'blet-e]

POST, TELECOMMUNICATIONS & MEDIA

stamp/letter	Briefmarke ['brief-maa-ke]/Brief [brief]
postcard	Postkarte ['posst-kaa-te]
I'm looking for a prepaid card for my mobile	Ich suche eine Prepaid-Karte für mein Handy [ikh 'zoo-khe 'ei-ne 'pre-paid-kaa-te für mein 'hen-dee]
Do I need a special area code?	Brauche ich eine spezielle Vorwahl? ['brow-khe ikh 'ei-ne shpets-ee-'ell-e 'fore-vaal]
Where can I find internet access?	Wo finde ich einen Internetzugang? [vo 'fin-de ikh 'ei-nen 'in-ter-net-tsoo-gang]
socket/adapter/ charger/wi-fi	Steckdose ['shtek-doh-ze]/Adapter [a-'dap-te]/ Ladegerät ['laa-de-ge-rayt]/WLAN ['vay-laan]

LEISURE, SPORTS & BEACH

bike/scooter rental	Fahrrad-['faa-raat]/Mofa-Verleih ['mo-fa fer-lei]
rental shop	Vermietladen [fer-'meet-laa-den]
lesson	Übungsstunde ['ü-bungs-shtun-de]

NUMBERS

0 null [null]	10 zehn [tsayn]	20 zwanzig ['tsvantsikh]
1 eins [eins]	11 elf [elf]	50 Fünfzig ['fünf-tsikh]
2 zwei [tsvei]	12 zwölf [tsvölf]	100 (ein) Hundert ['hun-dert]
3 drei [drei]	13 dreizehn [' dreitsayn]	200 Zwei Hundert [tsvei 'hun-dert]
4 vier [feer]	14 vierzehn ['feertsayn]	1000 (ein) Tausend ['tow-zent]
5 fünf [fünf]	15 fünfzehn ['fünftsayn]	2000 Zwei Tausend [tsvei 'tow-zent]
6 sechs [zex]	16 sechzehn ['zekhtsayn]	10 000 Zehn Tausend [tsayn 'tow-zent]
7 sieben ['zeeben]	17 siebzehn ['zeebtsayn]	
8 acht [akht]	18 achtzehn ['akhtsayn]	½ ein halb [ein halp]
9 neun [noyn]	19 neunzehn ['noyntsayn]	¼ ein viertel [ein 'feer-tel]

NOTES

MARCO POLO TRAVEL GUIDES

ALGARVE
AMSTERDAM
ANDALUCÍA
ATHENS
AUSTRALIA
AUSTRIA
BALI
  LOMBOK,
  GILI ISLANDS
BANGKOK
BARCELONA
BERLIN
BRAZIL
BRUGES, GHENT &
  ANTWERP
BRUSSELS
BUDAPEST
BULGARIA
CALIFORNIA
CAMBODIA
CANADA EAST
CANADA WEST
  ROCKIES
CAPE TOWN
  WINE LANDS,
  GARDEN ROUTE
CAPE VERDE
CHANNEL ISLANDS
CHICAGO
  & THE LAKES
CHINA
COLOGNE
COPENHAGEN
CORFU
COSTA BLANCA
  VALENCIA
COSTA BRAVA
  BARCELONA
COSTA DEL SOL
  GRANADA
CRETE
CUBA
CYPRUS
  NORTH AND
  SOUTH
DRESDEN
DUBAI
DUBLIN
DUBROVNIK &
  DALMATIAN COAST

EDINBURGH
EGYPT
EGYPT'S RED
  SEA RESORTS
FINLAND
FLORENCE
FLORIDA
FRENCH ATLANTIC
  COAST
FRENCH RIVIERA
  NICE, CANNES &
  MONACO
FUERTEVENTURA
GRAN CANARIA
GREECE
HAMBURG
HONG KONG
  MACAU
ICELAND
INDIA
INDIA SOUTH
  GOA & KERALA
IRELAND
ISRAEL
ISTANBUL
ITALY
JORDAN
KOS
KRAKOW
LAKE GARDA

LANZAROTE
LAS VEGAS
LISBON
LONDON
LOS ANGELES
MADEIRA
  PORTO SANTO
MADRID
MALLORCA
MALTA
  GOZO
MAURITIUS
MENORCA
MILAN
MONTENEGRO
MOROCCO
MUNICH
NAPLES &
  THE AMALFI COAST
NEW YORK
NEW ZEALAND
NORWAY
OSLO
PARIS
PHUKET
PORTUGAL
PRAGUE

RHODES
ROME
SAN FRANCISCO
SARDINIA
SCOTLAND
SEYCHELLES
SHANGHAI
SICILY
SINGAPORE
SOUTH AFRICA
SRI LANKA
STOCKHOLM
SWITZERLAND
TENERIFE
THAILAND
TURKEY
TURKEY
  SOUTH COAST
TUSCANY
UNITED ARAB
  EMIRATES
USA SOUTHWEST
VENICE
VIENNA
VIETNAM
ZÁKYNTHOS

- PACKED WITH INSIDER TIPS
- BEST WALKS AND TOURS
- FULL-COLOUR PULL-OUT MAP
  AND STREET ATLAS

STREET ATLAS

The green line ▬▬ indicates the Walking tours (p. 106–111)

All tours are also marked on the pull-out map

Photo: The Federal Chancellery

Charlotten-
burg

Wilmersdorf

130

(Bez.CH-WI)

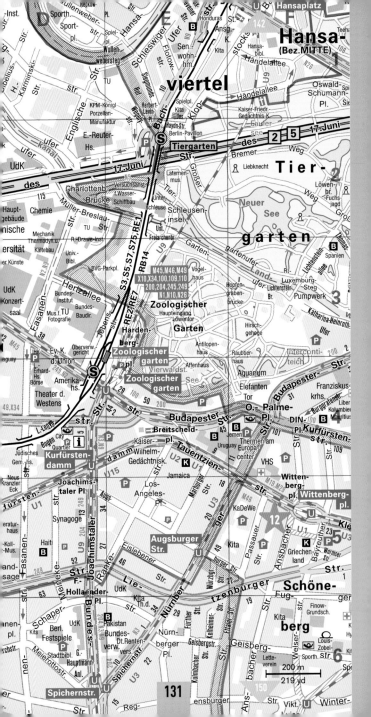

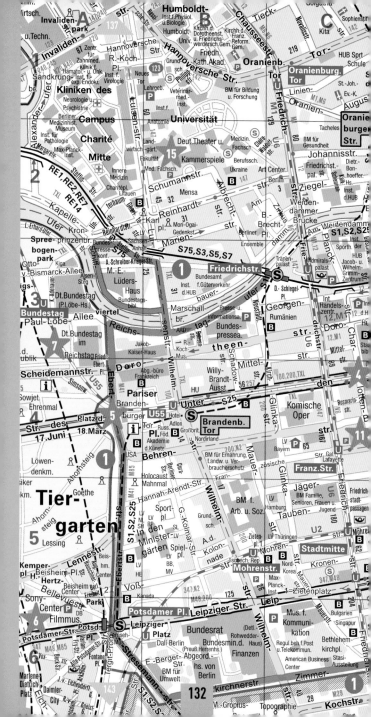

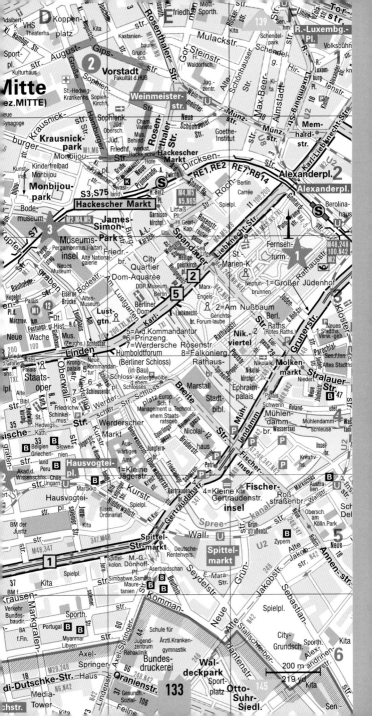

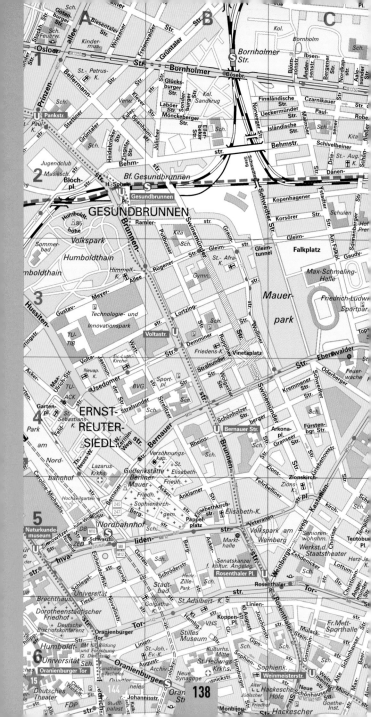

Königin
Elisabeth
Herzberge
(KEH)

LICHTENBERG

1 Bidenswinkel
2 Silberweidenweg
3 Freesienweg
4 Heidenelkenweg

Hyperboloid projection
(magnifying glass effect)
Change of scale from the
inner city to the outlying districts

BVG
Betriebs-
hof

1 Nibelungenring   Zentral-
2 Rumoldstraße   friedhof
3 Alzeyweg
4 Giselherstrid
5 Hadburgpfad

Lichtenberg

Amt
f. Umwelt
u. Natur

Müllers Ruh   Gotlinde

193   OE25,60
            RB12·NE26

Friedrichs-
felde

S   FURTER

B. LICHTENBERG
RB12·24·NE26
OE25,60
256

ALT-FRIEDRICHS-
FELDE

S5,7,75

Güterbf.

U5   Grüner
            Grund
FRIEDRICHS-
FELDE

Lichtenberg

NÖLDNER
PLATZ

Neuap.K.

RUMMELSBURGER   STR

Friedrichs-

NÖLDNER

S   S3   LUCK

1 SCHLICHT-
ALLEE
KI
Paradies   Sanssouci

SEWAN   felde

Rummelsburg

BETRIEBSBF
RUMMELSBG.

1 Dolgenseestr.
2 Mellenseestr.

RE 3

1 Emma-Ihrer-Str.
2 Clara-Grunwald-Str.
3 Lina-Morgenstern-Str.
4 Alice- u. Hella-Hirsch-Ring
5 Paula-Fürst-Str.
6 Gisele-Freund-Hain
7 Charlotte-Salomon-Hain

Stralau

Bürger-
und
Tiefbauamt

Kowalke

Kraftwerk
Klingenberg

RE 1·2·7 RB14

1094 yd

S3

Plänter-
wald

Archenhold
Sternwarte

147

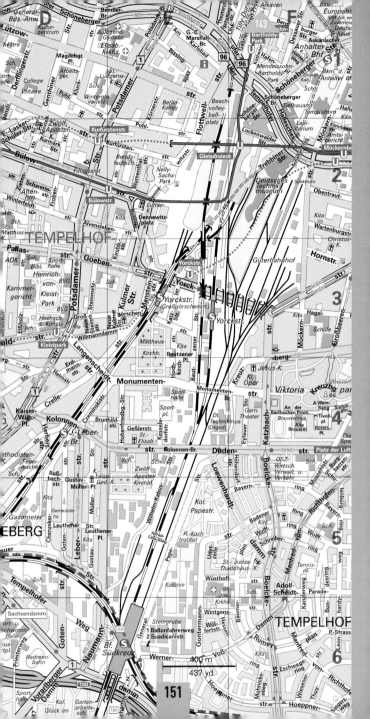

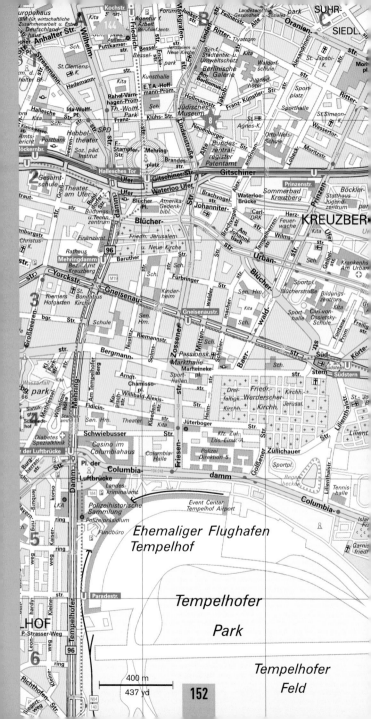

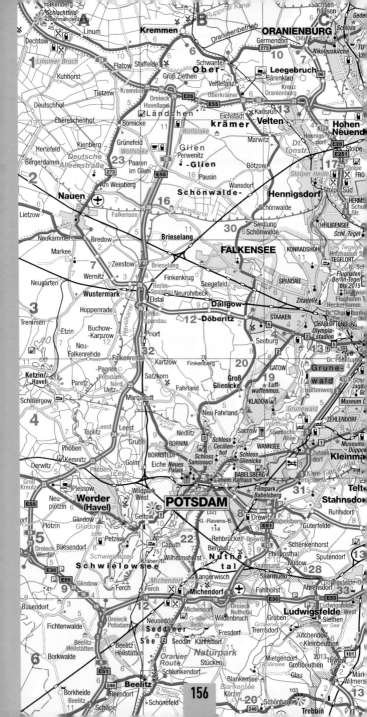

This index lists a selection of the streets and squares shown in the street atlas.

KEY TO STREET ATLAS

Motorway (Freeway) Autobahn		Autoroute Autostrada
Road with four lanes Vierspurige Straße		Route à quatre voies Strada a quattro corsie
Federal / trunk road Bundes-/ Fernstraße		Route fédérale / nationale Strada statale /di grande comunicazione
Main road Hauptstraße		Route principale Strada principale
Pedestrian zone - One way road Fußgängerzone - Einbahnstraße		Zone piétonne - Rue à sens unique Zona pedonale - Via a senso unico
Railway with station Eisenbahn mit Bahnhof		Chemin de fer avec gare Ferrovia con stazione
Underground (railway) U-Bahn		Métro Metropolitana
Bus-route - Tramway Buslinie - Straßenbahn		Ligne d'autocar - Tram Linea d'autobus - Tram
Information - Youth hostel Information - Jugendherberge		Information - Auberge de jeunesse Informazioni - Ostello della gioventù
Church - Church of interest Kirche - Sehenswerte Kirche		Église - Église remarquable Chiesa - Chiesa di notevole interesse
Synagogue - Mosque Synagoge - Moschee		Synagogue - Mosquée Sinagoga - Moschea
Police station - Post office Polizeistation - Postamt		Poste de police - Bureau de poste Posto di polizia - Ufficio postale
Hospital Krankenhaus		Hôpital Ospedale
Monument - Radio or TV tower Denkmal - Funk- oder Fernsehturm		Monument - Tour d'antennes Monumento - Pilone radio o TV
Theatre - Taxi rank Theater - Taxistand		Théâtre - Station taxi Teatro - Posteggio di tassí
Fire station - School Feuerwache - Schule		Poste de pompiers - École Guardia del fuoco - Scuola
Open air -/ Indoor swimming pool Freibad - Hallenbad		Piscine en plein air - Piscine couverte Piscina all'aperto - Piscina coperta
Public toilet - Restaurant Öffentliche Toilette - Ausflugslokal		Toilette publique - Restaurant Gabinetto pubblico - Ristorante
Indoor car park - Car park Parkhaus - Parkplatz		Parking couvert - Parking Autosilo - Area di parcheggio
Stadtspaziergänge Walking tours		Promenades en ville Passeggiate urbane
MARCO POLO Highlight		MARCO POLO Highlight

Visit Berlin's Origins.

And shoot the dragon! St. George's deadly battle is one of Berlin's most frequently photographed statues.

The Nikolaiviertel is the historic centre of Berlin. It brings together Berlin's shortest alleyway, "the most beautiful spot in Berlin", and the first and oldest church in the city, four other museums, architecture stretching back over eight centuries, a historic trail with nineteen information points winding its way through the entire quarter; numerous sculptures, countless photo opportunities, twenty-four cafés and restaurants, and twice as many shops, plus lots more.

The Nikolaiviertel and its pedestrianised alleyways are a great place to spend a day – no matter what the weather!

NIKOLAI VIERTEL 1237

INDEX

This index lists all sights, museums and places, plus the names of important people featured in this guide. Numbers in bold indicate a main entry.

CREDITS

WRITE TO US

e-mail: info@marcopologuides.co.uk

Did you have a great holiday?
Is there something on your mind?
Whatever it is, let us know!
Whether you want to praise, alert us
to errors or give us a personal tip –
MARCO POLO would be pleased to
hear from you.
We do everything we can to provide the
very latest information for your trip.

Nevertheless, despite all of our authors'
thorough research, errors can creep in.
MARCO POLO does not accept any
liability for this. Please contact us by
e-mail or post.

MARCO POLO Travel Publishing Ltd
Pinewood, Chineham Business Park
Crockford Lane, Chineham
Basingstoke, Hampshire RG24 8AL
United Kingdom

PICTURE CREDITS
Cover photograph: Brandenburger Tor (istockphoto: Nikada); cyclist (Corbis/Terra: Stefano Amantini)
Corbis/Terra: Stefano Amantini (1 top); DuMont Bildarchiv: Freyer (72 r.), Specht (3 top, 8, 59, 76/77, 111, 112, 115);
eROCKIT GmbH; Stefan Gulas, Sascha Nolte (17 top); Freies Museum Berlin (16 bottom); R. Freyer (2 centre top, 3 centre,
7, 15, 30, 36, 38/39, 52, 60, 66, 72 l., 86/87, 91, 92, 97, 106/107, 112/113, 113, 114, 114/115, 118 top, 118 bottom,
124/125); R. M. Gill (55); J. Gläser (40, 69); Huber: Mehlig (18/19); istockphoto (1 top); G. Knoll (2 bottom, 3 bottom,
64/65, 75, 98/99, 100, 104); Laif: Akhtar (70), Danner (84), Galli (95), Hahn (24 top), Herve CHAMPOLLION (6),
Westrich (2 top, 4, 5, 25); Laif/GAFF: Geilert (21); Look: Johaentges (57), Travelstock 44 (24 bottom); Look: Wothe (12);
mauritius images: Alamy (Klappe r., 10/11, 42, 45, 63, 81, 82), Eisen (48), Otto (23), Scott (88), Thormaehlen (103);
mauritius images/imagebroker: Henkelmann (119), Reister (34/35), Steiner (50), Wrba (46/47); Mamo Falafel:
Stefan Pramme (16 top); Smiling Berlin Verlag: Lasse Walter (17 bottom); O. Stadler (Klappe l.); M. Weigt (2 centre
bottom, 9, 26/27, 73, 78, 109); www.slackliner-berlin.de: Markus Altmann (16 centre)

2nd Edition – revised and updated 2014
Worldwide Distribution: Marco Polo Travel Publishing Ltd, Pinewood, Chineham Business Park,
Crockford Lane, Basingstoke, Hampshire RG24 8AL, United Kingdom. Email: sales@marcopolouk.com
© MAIRDUMONT GmbH & Co. KG, Ostfildern
Chief editor: Marion Zorn
Author: Christine Berger, Editor: Jochen Schürmann
Programme supervision: Ann-Katrin Kutzner, Nikolai Michaelis, Silwen Randebrock
Picture editor: Gabriele Forst
What's hot: wunder media, Munich
Cartography street atlas: © MAIRDUMONT, Ostfildern
Cartography pull-out map: © MAIRDUMONT, Ostfildern
Design: milchhof : atelier, Berlin;
Front cover, pull-out map cover, page 1: factor product munich
Translated from the German by Robert McInnes; editor of the English edition: Christopher Wynne
Phrase book in cooperation with Ernst Klett Sprachen GmbH, Stuttgart, Editorial by Pons Wörterbücher
Printed in China

DOS & DON'TS 👆

A few things you should avoid

DON'T FALL FOR STREET GAMBLERS

Groups of men – often from Eastern Europe – delude unsuspecting people into thinking that it is the easiest thing in the world to win at a game of 'thimbles'. Three matchboxes, cups or other objects – one of which has a bead, pea or ball hidden under it – are moved back at forth at great speed and the player has to guess where the ball is. Standard bets of 50 euros are taken – and there is a dead certainty that you will lose. Don't be fooled by other players who seem to be winning; they are all members of the gang.

DON'T DRIVE INTO THE CITY

Anybody who doesn't have four big suitcases, ten shopping bags and three poodles to drag through the city can easily do without a car. A lack of knowledge about the city, traffic jams and the lack of – or extremely expensive – parking spaces can quickly take all the fun out of your holiday. If you want to get around Berlin independently and flexibly, the reliable underground, district line, tram and bus networks will prove to be ideal.

DON'T BUY SMUGGLED CIGARETTES

Berlin is a great place for bargain-hunter: however, a packet of cigarettes bought at half price from a Vietnamese dealer is not really a good deal. These are illegally smuggled goods and buyers can also be punished by law.

DON'T DODGE FARES

Never forget to stamp your ticket! Berlin ticket inspectors like their job: they are inconspicuous in their everyday clothes and extremely diligent and merciless when they catch a fare-dodger in the underground or anywhere else. If you're caught, you will have to pay 40 euros! The best thing is to buy a weekly ticket or use a Welcome Card (see Practical Information).

DON'T TRAVEL BY TAXI WITHOUT A MAP

Be prepared that not all taxi drivers know the city or individual districts like the back of their hand. Passengers often have to tell taxi drivers where to go – especially in the more outlying areas. The best thing to do is to check the route on your map before you get into a taxi.

DON'T LEAVE YOUR BAGS UNATTENDED

Unfortunately, Berlin is a lucrative spot for pickpockets. The expert criminals make a big haul in stations, on escalators and in the hustle-and-bustle at large events. It is a good idea not to keep your wallet or purse in your hip or coat pocket, and always keep an eye on your handbag.

Ⓢ Ⓤ Bahn Berlin Liniennetz *Routemap*

Ⓢ
- S1 Potsdam Hbf ↔ Oranienburg
- S2 Blankenfelde ↔ Bernau
- S25 Teltow Stadt ↔ Hennigsdorf
- S3 Erkner ↔ Ostkreuz
- S41 Ring ↻ *im Uhrzeigersinn*
- S42 Ring ↺ *gegen Uhrzeigersinn*
- S45 Flughafen Berlin-Schönefeld ↔ Südkreuz (↔ Bundesplatz)
- S46 Königs Wusterhausen ↔ Westend
- S47 Königs Wusterhausen ↔ Südkreuz
- S5 Spindlersfeld ↔ Hermannstr.
- S6 Spindlersfeld ↔ Schöneweide
- S7 Strausberg Nord ↔ Spandau
- S75 Wartenberg ↔ Westkreuz
- S8 Wartenberg ↔ Lichtenberg (Zeuthen ↔) Grünau ↔ Birkenwerder
- S85 (Grünau ↔) Schöneweide (Grünau ↔) Pankow ↔ Birkenwerder
- S9 Waidmannslust (nur Mo-Fri) *(only Mon-Fri)*
- S9 Flughafen Berlin-Schönefeld ↔ Pankow
- S9 Flughafen Berlin-Schönefeld ↔ Treptower Park

Ⓤ
- U1 Warschauer Straße ↔ Uhlandstraße
- U2 Pankow ↔ Ruhleben
- U3 Nollendorfplatz ↔ Krumme Lanke
- U4 Nollendorfplatz ↔ Innsbrucker Platz
- U55 Hönow ↔ Alexanderplatz
- U5 Brandenburger Tor ↔ Hauptbahnhof
- U6 Alt-Tegel ↔ Alt-Mariendorf
- U7 Rathaus Spandau ↔ Rudow
- U8 Wittenau ↔ Hermannstraße
- U9 Osloer Straße ↔ Rathaus Steglitz

S+U-Bahn-Nachtverkehr
nur Fr/Sa. 0:30-5:30 Uhr
Sa/So und vor Feiertagen ca. 0:30-7:00 Uhr
S+U-Bahn nighttime traffic
Fri/Sat ca. 0:30 am-5:30 am
Sat/Sun and prior to holidays
ca. 0:30 am-7:00 am

Wittenberge RE6 RB5 Kremmen
Stralsund/RE5 Rostock

Vehlefanz
Bärenklau
Velten (Mark)
Hohen Neuendorf West
Hennigsdorf
Heiligensee
Schulzendorf
Tegel Rath
U6 Alt-Tegel
Borsigwerke
Holzhauser Str.
Eichbornd
Otisstr.
Scharnweberstr.
Kurt-Schumacher-Platz
X9 128
✈ Tegel TXL
X9 TXL X9 109 128
Afrikanische
Re
TXL 128
X9 109
TXL
X9 TXL
Beusselstr.
Jungfernheide
X9 109

Nauen RB10 RB14
RB21 Wismar
Brieselang
Finkenkrug
Falkensee
Seegefeld
Albrechtshof
Dallgow-Döberitz Elstal
Staaken Spandau S5 S9 RB13
RE4-RB13 Rathenow RE4 Wuster-mark RB10 RB21

Siemens-stadt
Zitadelle Haselhorst Paulsternstr. Rohrdamm damm Halemweg
Altstadt Spandau
Jakob-Kaiser-Platz
X9 54Pl
Rathaus Spandau U7 U2
RE2-RE4-RE6-RB10-RB14
Stresow
Ruhleben
U2 RB14
Pichelsberg
Olympia-Stadion
Olympiastadion
Neu-Westend
Kaiserdamm
Heerstr.
Theodor-Heuss-Platz
Messe Nord/ ICC
Messe ZOB ICC
Messe Süd
Sophie-Charlotte-Platz
Wilmers-dorfer Str.
Bismarckstr.
Deutsche Oper
Savignyplatz
Tie
Ernst-Re Pla

Westend
Mierendorffplatz
Richard-Wagner-Platz

Westkreuz
S75
Charlotten-burg
Halensee
Grunewald
Adenauer-platz
Konstanzer Str.
Uhlandstr.
U1 U3
Kurfürsten-damm
Spichernstr.
Hohenzollern-platz
Fehrbelliner Platz
Blissestr.
Be
B

Hohenzollerndamm
Heidelberger Platz
Rüdesheimer Platz
Breitenbachplatz
Podbielskiallee
Dahlem-Dorf
Thielplatz
Oskar-Helene-Heim
Onkel Toms Hütte
Schlachtensee
Krumme Lanke
U3
Mexikoplatz
Friedrich-Wilhelm-Platz
Walther-Schreiber-Platz
Schloßstr.
Bundesplatz S45
Rathaus Steglitz U9 U9
Botanischer Garten
Lichterfelde West

Nikolassee
Zehlendorf Sundgauer Str.
Wannsee S1 S7 RB22
Priort
Marquardt
Golm
Branden-burg RE1
Magde-burg RE1
Werder (Havel)
Pirschheide
Caputh-Geltow
Caputh-Schwielowsee
Ferch-Lienewitz

Park Sans-souci
Char-lotten-hof
Griebnitz-see
Babelsberg
Potsdam Hbf
S1 S7 RB21
Medienstadt Babelsberg
Rehbrücke
Wilhelmshorst
Saarmund
Michendorf
Seddin
Ludwigsfelde-Struveshof
Dessau RE7   Jüterbog
S25 S26 Teltow Stadt
Lichterfelde

Lichterfelde
Ludwig
Thyrow
Birke
Jüterbog RE3 RE4 Lutherstad